WITH

MUSLIM POLITICS IN INDIA

INDIAN SECULAR FORUM

MUSLIM POLITICS
IN INDIA

by

HAMID DALWAI

FOREWORD
by
A. B. SHAH

NACHIKETA

NACHIKETA PUBLICATIONS
280 Sleater Road, Bombay 7

First published November 1968

Reprinted January 1969

Set in 8 and 10 point Linotype Caledonia face

PRINTED IN INDIA

PRINTED BY MOHAN G. SHIRALI AT MOHAN MUDRANALAYA, ACME ESTATE, SEWRI (EAST), BOMBAY 15 AND PUBLISHED BY A. B. SHAH FOR NACHIKETA PUBLICATIONS, 4 JOOTHICA, 280 SLEATER ROAD, BOMBAY 7

To
Jawaharlal Nehru

CONTENTS

I am no more than man: when I order you anything respecting religion, receive it; and when I order you anything about the affairs of the world, then I am nothing more than man.

THE PROPHET MUHAMMAD

FOREWORD

*Men of Athens! If you were to release me on the condition
that I should stop teaching the youth, I would still continue
my teachings in spite of every threat that hangs over me.*
—Socrates

Mr Hamid Dalwai's emergence during the last two years
as one of the most thought-provoking critics of Muslim
attitudes marks in my opinion an important turning point
in the history of Muslim politics in India. For the first time
since the foundation of the Central National Moham-
medan Association by Syed Ameer Ali in 1877, a Muslim
student of the problem is approaching it from a standpoint that is neither Hindu nor Muslim, neither Gandhian
nor Marxist. Mr Dalwai's standpoint is, rather, that of a
student of history and culture, and his views are expressed
with a kind of courage and forthrightness that is rare
among Indian secularists. In doing so, he is aware that
he is running a great personal risk. Already he has received letters threatening dire consequences, including death,
for him and the members of his family, and his old parents
in the Konkan have already been subjected to ostracism,
including the denial of services by the village functiona-
ries.

Why does Mr Dalwai continue taking this risk, when no
educated Muslim is prepared even to court simple un-
pleasantness by telling to his co-religionists the truths

9

that he is convinced of? To ask the question is, however,
to answer it. It is precisely because educated Muslims prefer playing safe even though that would mean pandering
to the prejudices and superstitions of their less fortunate
brethren that Mr Dalwai is engaged in what may be called
a one-man crusade against the obscurantism of Muslim
society in India. Uncharitable critics are convinced that
he is out to court the favour of communalist Hindus. If
only these critics had read Mr Dalwai's writings in full—
and they are not very voluminous as this small book shows
—or discussed the question with him, perhaps they would
have reacted in a different way. Not that they would have
necessarily agreed with him, but a dialogue could have
started between Mr Dalwai and his friends on the one
hand, and their critics on the other. What has actually
happened is that Mr Dalwai has stirred up a hornets' nest
round his head among the educated Muslims of India and
their fellow-travellers among the Hindus. At the same
time, those among the communalist Hindus who in the
beginning imagined that they had got a Muslim recruit
for fighting their battles were sorely disappointed when
they discovered that Mr Dalwai was equally opposed to the
obscurantism of any community and of any type. It may
come as a surprise to Muslims and non-communalist Hindus that an attempt was made to break up, through stone-
throwing, a public meeting that Mr Dalwai was addres-
sing at Nagpur in October last. Mr Dalwai is satisfied that
the stones did not come from Muslims.

However, perhaps it is not quite fair to blame all Mr
Dalwai's Muslim critics. He has so far written in Marathi
and most educated Muslims of Maharashtra, particularly
those in Bombay, do not know the language. Under the
circumstances, they prefer to judge him on the basis of
gossip and 'free' translation into English by someone who

knows Marathi. Some have even passed a verdict on him
on the basis of how he sits or stands in company!

I am therefore happy that the Indian Secular Forum is
bringing out this authoritative version of Mr Dalwai's articles in a language that is still the effective link language
of India. The Forum also hopes to bring out or sponsor
Urdu and Hindi versions of this book.

II

I shall not try to summarize Mr Dalwai's views in this
foreword, for the simple reason that I am in almost total
agreement with him. I would rather mention here the central point of his argument and elaborate it with a view
to bringing out its significance.

Mr Dalwai's thesis is that the basic malaise of Muslim
society (in India as elsewhere with the exception of Turkey
and perhaps Tunisia) lies in the fact that it has never had
a renaissance in its entire history of more than thirteen
hundred years. All other problems, including that of its
secular and democratic integration in the larger Indian
society, are derivative in character. In the absence of such
intergation, what has come to be known as the Hindu-
Muslim problem cannot be solved. However, the type of
integration that is necessary here cannot be achieved unless Muslims no less than Hindus learn to separate religion
from the rights and obligations of citizenship of a modern
state. And only those can promote such integration who
themselves are committed to the values of an open society
and to the outlook on man and the universe that is sanc-
tioned by science and scientific method. Others can at best
play a passive role, if not obstruct the process of integration. If one accepts this view of the problem, one cannot
help feeling that Integration Committees appointed by

Governments are not likely to accomplish anything worth the name. For instance, the Committee appointed by the Government of Maharashtra includes among its members not only representatives of all political parties but also of the Majlis-e-Mushawarat, whose leaders do not believe in Hindu-Muslim co-operation for fighting communalism (see M. A. Karandikar's letter 'Muslims & India' in *The Times of India*, Bombay, November 11, 1968). Indeed, the Committee is so large—it has sixty members—that it could have easily been made completely representative by adding a Naxalite communist and a member of the R.S.S!

It is clear that good intentions are not enough for lesser men to solve problems where one like Gandhi could not succeed. Hindu-Muslim unity and the abolition of untouchability were two of the most important elements of his programme for the freedom and regeneration of India. In a sense they were among the pre-conditions of *Swaraj* as he visualized it, and therefore he often described their attainment as even more important than the withdrawal of British power from India. He succeeded in considerable measure in his fight against untouchability. Though much remains to be done, no Hindu except the lunatic fringe represented by the Shankaracharya of Puri[1] would have a moment's hesitation in supporting measures designed to bring about the complete liquidation of untouchability. However, Hindu-Muslim unity evaded Gandhi throughout his active life in India except for a brief spell during the Khilafat agitation.[2] Not only that;

[1] In April 1968 during a *Gita Pravachan* week at Ahmedabad the Shankaracharya defended the organizers' arrangements for segregating Harijans from the caste Hindus in the audience. *Cf.* also his views expressed in *Kalyan* (Hindi), October, November 1967.

[2] And the Muslim inspiration behind this short-lived unity was

in spite of Gandhi's ceaseless effort the country had to accept partition as the price of freedom. And soon after Independence Gandhi had to die at the hands of a Hindu fanatic, though he alone among the leaders of the Indian National Congress was unreconciled to partition.

Why did this happen? How was it that Gandhi who advised the Hindus to be patient and generous to the Muslims, and who asked the British to hand over power to Jinnah if they so preferred but quit, came to be increasingly isolated not only from the Muslims but even from his own followers in his quest for unity? And how is it that twenty-one years after partition the Hindu-Muslim problem is still with us, in the sense that we are still groping even for a valid theoretical solution?

A satisfactory discussion of these questions would require an examination of Gandhi's philosophy of life, his theory of social change and, most important of all, the nature of the Hindu and Islamic traditions and the types of mind that they mould. All this cannot be undertaken in the space of a foreword and must wait for a later date. Here I shall only deal with some of these questions and that, too, to the extent that is necessary for indicating the lines on which further discussion may usefully proceed.

III

Gandhi was essentially a philosophical anarchist in his view of man and did not subscribe to the idea of original sin. On the contrary, he believed that man was 'essentially' good, for every human being had a spark of the

not that of secular territorial nationalism but of an extra-territorial loyalty based on religion. For some interesting sidelights on this question, *cf.* Ram Gopal, *Indian Muslims*, Asia Publishing House, Bombay 1959, 1964.

divine in him and no one was beyond redemption even
though the struggle for self-realization was bound to be
arduous and long. He therefore approached the problem
of Hindu-Muslim unity as a well-meaning, persuasive, non-
sectarian nationalist. He worked on the assumption, based
on his experience in South Africa, that if only Hindus and
Muslims could be brought together in joint constructive
endeavour, they would see that unity was in their common
interest and learn to live together in peace and harmony.
To this end he sought to project the universal human
values preached by all major religions including Hinduism
and Islam, and hoped that in the course of time the forces of unity would triumph over those of separatism. For,
according to Gandhi's way of thinking, 'true' religion could
only join, not keep separate, men of different faiths. If
Hindus and Muslims in India regarded themselves as essentially separate groups the fault, Gandhi thought, lay
not in the beliefs and practices enjoined by their scriptures
but in a defective understanding of their 'real' message.

This is a noble view of man and religion. But it overlooks the fact that man, as a product of evolution, is a
union of good and evil, just as it overlooks the historically
determined character of his culture and institutions. Consequently, Gandhi missed the deeper socio-historical
and cultural roots of the religious conflict in India. Instead,
he attributed its origin to the wily British, who certainly
were interested in keeping the Muslims away from the
'seditious' and 'Hindu' nationalist movement.[4] Gandhi was
satisfied that if only there were enough goodwill on the
part of a sufficient number of Hindus and Muslims, sooner

---

[4] *cf.* Ram Gopal, *op. cit.*, and Bal Gangadhar Tilak, *Articles from
'Kesari'* (Marathi), vol I, Kesari-Maratha Sanstha, Poona 1922 for
evidence from late nineteenth and early twentieth century records
and examples of British policy of *divide et impera*.

or later they would realize the suicidal implications of religious conflict and work together for the attainment of freedom from foreign rule. This approach, which I would call the Rama-Rahim approach because it postulated the peaceful coexistence of Hindus and Muslims without any fundamental modification of their attitude to religion, was bound to fail. It did not take into account the hold that religion with its dogma, tradition, custom and ritual has on the minds of men in a pre-modern society. Also, it presupposed that the logic of individual or small-group behaviour could be applied to huge, faceless masses whose only common bond is blind loyalty to a tribal collectivity in the sacred name of God and religion.

This is another way of saying that the Gandhian approach was saintly in the main. It was also akin to the Marxist, in the sense that it assigned a derivative role to the cultural factor. Gandhi believed that the urge for freedom would enable the Muslims to take an enlightened view of their religion. This, however, presupposes that a certain measure of individuation has already taken place in the culture system known as Islam, and Gandhi assumed that it had. The Hindu mind is essentially individualistic, indeed narcissistic [5], so that it is easy for it to transcend intermediate loyalties and take to the path of individual salvation. This has its disadvantages as well as advantages, and perhaps the former outweigh the latter. The point is that it is difficult for a Hindu to visualize, except by a special effort of reason and the imagination, a mind that is almost totally lacking in the conception of the individual and derives the significance of human life solely from

[5] *cf.* P. Spratt, *Hindu Culture and Personality*, P. C. Manaktala and Sons, Bombay 1966. See also, 'Tradition and Modernity in India' in A. B. Shah, *Planning for Democracy and Other Essays*, P. C. Manaktala and Sons, Bombay 1967.

the individual's membership of a collectivity. This, however, seems to be a characteristic feature of almost all cul-
tures based on revealed religion. If Christian culture appears to be different in this respect, that is because almost
from its inception Christianity was influenced by the Greek
tradition. It was the revival of the Greek tradition that
led to the Renaissance and the rise of Protestantism with
its stress on personal interpretation of the Holy Writ. The
humanization of Christianity, with the consequent growth
of a secular conception of individuality, was thus a direct
outcome of its interaction with the Greek tradition.[6] It is
worth noting in this connection that unlike the People of
the Book, the Greeks were not blessed with a prophet
nor, unlike the Hindus, with an incarnation of God. They
had therefore to rely on reason and observation alone for
discovering the nature of things. Also, they were poly-
theist and their gods were hardly distinguishable from
human beings with superhuman powers but entirely non-
transcendental interests. Consequently, the Greeks could
develop a tradition of critical inquiry and a climate of
tolerance necessary to let 'a hundred schools contend' and
'a hundred flowers bloom'. They had also another advantage. They had no counterpart of the Vedas, which the
Hindus regarded as eternal and uncreated by man. Unlike
the Hindus, they were therefore free from the burden of
unchanging Truth and able to create science as quest and
the idea of scientific method as providing a tool of inquiry

---

[6] A secular attitude to the state was, during its early years, in-
dispensable for Christianity to survive in the hostile atmosphere of
a well-established Roman state. What the Renaissance did was to
revive this attitude and to extend it from the state to the individual.
It would be interesting to speculate on the lines along which
Christianity would have developed if, like Muhammad, Jesus too
had founded a state.

as well as a criterion for the validity of its findings.

The Greek tradition might have had a similar effect on Islam too. But by the time Islam came in contact with it—in the reign of al-Mamun (813-833)—the latter had already lost its elan and Islam too had outgrown its formative stage. More important still, Islam arose in a society that was riven with inter-tribal feuds, had no state worth the name and did not hesitate to subject dissent to crude tribal persecution. The founder of Islam had therefore also to found a state before its message was fully delivered, let alone developed in contact with a more advanced culture without the arbitrament of force. The rapid and spectacular expansion of Islam during the hundred years following the death of the Prophet over the stagnant and often decadent societies of the surrounding region also had an inhibitory effect on its future development. For continued victory over others strengthened the Muslim's conviction that his faith was not only perfect but superior to others and its doctrine, infallible. Dissent, when it arose, was as ruthlessly put down in Islam as in mediaeval Christianity, so that even the finest and most courageous of Muslim scholars were careful to avoid saying anything that might appear as questioning the fundamental tenets of the faith. Thus the Mutazilites, who made use of Greek ideas in the exposition and defence of Islamic theological doctrine, 'were regarded as heretical by the main body of Sunnite Muslims'[7] and were treated as such. Even Ibn Sina, one of the few really great Muslim philosophers, was criticized by authorities of the Muslim tradition for 'limiting the power of God to a predetermined logical structure' and for 'diminishing the sense of awe of the

[7] W. Montgomery Watt, *What is Islam?* Longmans, London 1968, p. 181. *Cf.* also G. E. von Grunebaum, *Mediaeval Islam*, (2nd edn), Chicago 1953, pp. 102-105.

finite before the infinite'.[8] Nor is that all. Ibn Sina himself in his later years seems to have turned—or posed as—
a devout gnostic. Indeed, 'it comes as something of a shock
to be confronted with the thickening web of "irrational"
elements in the writings of such a personality as Avicenna'.[9]

I have deliberately dwelt at some length on this aspect
of Islam as a cultural tradition. The reason is not that
Islam is unique in its record of intolerance in the past; it
is, rather, that Islam still exhibits the same intolerance of
free inquiry and dissent as it did in less enlightened
times.[10] What little possibility there might have been of
the softening of this attitude through the development of
science and philosophy after the mutual persecution of
the Mutazillites and their orthodox opponents was effectively destroyed by al-Ghazali (d. 1,111) for centuries to
come. His work ensured that no renaissance would ever
take place in Muslim society unless, as in Turkey, it were
imposed from above. Muslim scholars look upon al-Ghazali
as the greatest thinker that Islamic culture has produced.
I am inclined to believe that he was the greatest disaster
that befell it since the death of the Prophet.

So great has been the hold of orthodoxy on the Muslim
mind that nowhere has Muslim society so far been able
to throw up an articulate class of liberal Muslims committed to modern values and all that such a commitment
means in various fields of life. Such a class can alone subject the tradition of Islam to a critical scrutiny and pre-
pare the ground for the entry of Muslim society into the

---

[8] Seyyed Hossein Nasr, *An Introduction to Islamic Cosmological
Doctrines*, Harvard University Press, Cambridge, Mass. 1964, p. 214.

[9] H. A. R. Gibb in the *Preface* to S. H. Nasr, *op. cit.*

[10] *Cf.*, for instance, the recent resignation of Dr Fazl Rahman from
his post as Director of the Pakistan Government's Institute of Islamic Studies as a result of the *ulema*'s wrath against him.

modern age. For, as the experience of developing countries in the post-War period shows, efforts to modernize the political and economic systems in the absence of social and cultural modernization accompanying, if not preceding, them can only result in frustration or perversion.

That the issue is basic to the future of Muslim society is illustrated by the still unresolved conflict, characteristic of almost the entire Muslim world, between the conception of territorial nationalism and that of a politico-religious *ummat* that cuts across national boundaries. The repeated attempts of the Muslim Brotherhood to assassinate President Nasser in the name of Islam merely show that the conflict cannot be resolved until the very ethos of Islamic culture undergoes a qualitative change. To initiate a process that would bring about such a transformation is the historic task confronting educated Muslims everywhere in the world. There are signs of this happening in some of the countries—Pakistan, for example—where Muslims have to face the responsibility of running the state.

However, there are serious difficulties in their path, not the least of which is the self-contradictory situation in which politicians generally find themselves by trying to eat their cake and have it too. At home the demands of development often compel them to adopt policies, such as family planning and drastic modification of personal law, which cannot but provoke the wrath of the orthodox. At the same time, they do not hesitate to rouse and exploit the religious passions of their people when it suits their convenience, especially in international politics. Duplicity of this kind may prove useful for the time being but the price it exacts in the long run is likely to be out of all proportion to the gains. For instance, it inhibits the growth of genuinely critical, as distinguished from pedantic and apologetic, scholarship. The latter type of scholarship, of

which there is enough in the Muslim world, is generally
sterile, if not positively harmful, from the standpoint of
modernization. It is only the critical spirit that can release
the springs of creativity and wash away the debris of centuries.

The tragedy of Indian Muslims does not lie so much in
the backwardness of a vast majority of them in relation to
the Hindus—which is only a symptom—as in the unwilling-
ness of educated Muslims to undertake a critical reap-
praisal of their heritage. The cost would be insignificant
compared to what it would be in a country under Muslim
rule, or what their Hindu conterparts had to pay in the
preceding century. But the consciousness of a separate
identity or the desire to conform is unbelievably strong
among them. For instance, even an eminent scholar like
Professor M. Mujeeb finds it advisable to begin an otherwise magnificent work with the following obeisance to
orthodoxy: 'It is the author's firm belief that the Indian
Muslims have, in their religion of Islam, and in the true
(*sic*) representatives of the moral and spiritual values of
Islam the most reliable standards of judgement, and they
do not need to look elsewhere to discover how high or
low they stand'.[11] This is very much reminiscent of Hindu
pandits of the past, who began their treatises with an
invocation to God regardless of whether in subsequent
pages they were to deal with logic or mathematics, state-
craft or erotics.

IV

If Gandhi was guilty of the saint's fallacy and educated
Muslims of excessive group-consciousness or desire to con-

[11] M. Mujeeb, *The Indian Muslims*, George Allen & Unwin Ltd,
London 1967, p. 24.

form, the Marxists were guilty of over-simplification and false induction. They sought to interpret Hindu-Muslim relations in terms of economic interests and the machinations of the British. Gandhi as well as the Marxists assumed that the Muslim masses, as distinguished from their upper-class leadership, had at heart the same political and economic interests as their Hindu counterparts. They therefore concluded that as the struggle against political and economic injustice gathered momentum, the basis of Hindu-Muslim conflict would gradually be undermined. And once freedom was established and justice was on the march, the two communities would, it was hoped, begin to live in friendship and peace. In this perspective no critical examination of religion as a socio-cultural institution, let alone a frontal attack on some of the values and attitudes it sanctified, was considered necessary by either group.

That Gandhi should not have seen the need for such criticism is easy to understand. What is surprising is the attitude of those who swore by Marx. For the left arose as a standard-bearer of enlightenment and was as much a protest against religious obscurantism as against exploitation in the secular field. It is true that Indian Marxists were unsparing in their criticism of Hindu obscurantism. But that was relatively easy in view of the rather amorphous nature of Hinduism and the tradition of critical self-inquiry started by the reformers of the nineteenth century. There was no such tradition in Muslim society nor was there a large enough class of liberal, forward-looking Muslims which, like its Hindu counter-part in the preceding century, could initiate such a tradition. Consequently, Islam escaped the humanizing process through which Christianity in the West and, to a certain extent, Hinduism in India had to pass. Inspired by considerations that

were primarily political, the Marxists no less than the
Gandhians missed the true nature of the role that the doctrine and tradition of Islam played in the evolution of
Muslim politics in India. Gandhi made Khilafat a national
cause in order to win the confidence of Indian Muslims.
The Marxists were not particularly impressed by Gandhi's
support of the Khilafat agitation. But they too dared not
criticise Muslim communalism except in political terms,
whereas what was required was a thorough-going critique
of the philosophy and sociology of Islam of the type that
Marx considered 'the beginning of all criticism'. Even
M. N. Roy, who alone among Indian Marxists subjected
Hinduism to such an analysis, failed in this respect.

It is here that Mr Dalwai is breaking new ground,
though in an indirect way. His interest in the non-religious
aspects of Islam stems from his concern over the problem
of Hindu-Muslim relations and its bearing on our effort
to develop a modern and liberal society in India. He therefore does not deal with religion as such, or with Islam as
a religion, except insofar as religion is used as a cloak for
obscurantist and anti-humanist ends. It may therefore be
useful to consider here in brief the process by which all
religions come to be so used and defeat the inspiration
of their founders.

Every religion offers to its followers a vision of life and
a theory that incorporates this vision. In the history of
every religion, however, a stage arrives when the vision
fades into the background except for a socially ineffective
minority, and the theory achieves an absolute status un-
related to the historical situation in which it first arose.
When this happens religion proves a fetter on human freedom and creativity, superstition triumphs over science,
and ethics itself is perverted into a specious justification
of social inequities. Mediaeval Christianity and Hinduism

from classical times to the early years of the nineteenth century provide ample evidence for this view. The Renaissance humanized Christianity and Hinduism too underwent a partial but significant change of the same type in the nineteenth century. However, Islam still awaits its renaissance, and till it takes place Muslim society cannot be modernized nor can Muslims be integrated into a modern secular society, regardless of whether it is liberal or authoritarian.

The problem of Hindu-Muslim unity thus appears as an aspect of the larger problem of the modernization of Indian society. For, given the composition, past history and present context of this society, it would be unrealistic to imagine that the Hindu and the Muslim can live together as equal citizens unless each were willing to dissociate his political from his religious or cultural identity. For historical and other reasons, the Hindu is at an advantage in this respect. But precisely because of that, he has to accept the onus of promoting the modernization of Muslim society. So far, he has defaulted on this responsibility, apparently out of expediency but mainly because his own understanding of the task of modernization has been superficial and imitative. Consequently, well-meaning Hindus in public life have generally been soft-headed secularists in relation to Muslim society. Over the years their attitude has seriously damaged not only the cause of democratic secular integration but also the interests of Muslims themselves. It has created a vested interest in obscurantism, and encourages among educated Muslims a tendency to self-pity of the Mock Turtle kind instead of facilitating the emergence of a secular and forward-looking Muslim leadership. Worse still, in reaction to the persistent refusal, in the name of religion, of the spokesmen of Muslim society to meet the demands of the modern

conscience and the requirements of the modern age, a
growing number of well-meaning Hindus are rallying
under the banner of Hindu revivalism. Indeed, if the present trend continues unchecked, in a few years from now
most politically articulate Hindus and Muslims will be
confronting each other from platforms like those of the
R.S.S. and the Jamaat-e-Islami. One need not worry about
their fate—indeed, I would say to them: 'a plague on both
your houses!' But an overwhelming majority of the people of this country, be they Hindu or Muslim, are entitled
to a more decent society and its chances would suffer a
great set-back. That is why Mr Dalwai pleads that those
who speak in the name of secularism and democracy
should refuse to have any truck with obscurantist groups
claiming to represent the interests of Muslims even if it
means the loss of the Muslim vote for some years to come.
There are enough secular-minded Muslims, mostly of the
younger generation, who would like to establish rapport
with their Hindu counterparts. They feel alienated from
the bulk of their community and also from the Hindus
because of the latter's narcissistic attitude and short-sighted opportunism. Let secular Hindus seek them out and
give them a sense of belonging, not as Hindus or Muslims
but as fellow-citizens engaged in building an open society
in India.

I do not know to what extent Mr Dalwai will succeed
in persuading educated Muslims of the older generation
to look upon his approach with sympathy. But I know
from personal observation that he has succeeded in strik-
ing a chord in the hearts of younger Muslims, who seem
to be groping for new moorings in post-partition Indian
society. I also know that he has been able to give well-
meaning Hindus, particularly the idealistically motivated

members of the younger generation, a feeling that Hindu revivalism is no way of meeting the challenge of Muslim obscurantism. That also explains why those who believe that India should become a Hindu Rashtra have started having second thoughts about him. And if the younger generation of Hindus, who constitute nearly eighty-five per cent of the population of this country, can be prevented from turning obscurantist, what others think of Mr Dalwai is of little consequence for the future of secularism in India.

Bombay   A. B. SHAH
November 14, 1968   President, Indian Secular Forum

PREFACE

On January 24-25, 1968, *Sadhana*—a Marathi weekly published from Poona—had convened a seminar on the Hindu-
Muslim problem. These articles are based on notes for my
lecture in the seminar. *Sadhana* subsequently published
them in the form of four articles. To these, I have added
an article specially written for this English edition.

I am grateful to Professor A. B. Shah for the co-operation
he has given me in preparing this book for publication in
English translation, and I must also thank Mr Dilip Chitre
for translating the articles into English.

The Indian Secular Forum has sponsored the publication of this book and I am grateful to this organization
for all the assistance it has given me.

Bombay   HAMID DALWAI
November 14, 1968

1

HISTORICAL BACKGROUND

For the last two years I have been writing and speaking in public on the Hindu-Muslim communal problem in India. My analysis of the problem has had a mixed reception. Now that I am publishing my articles in the form of a book, I would like to explain my views in some detail to my readers—both Hindu and Muslim. And I also have to make an appeal to them.

It is obvious why the Muslim reaction to my views should be as adverse as it is. It is also understandable why the Hindus have generally welcomed my views, although there are some Hindus who believe that my articles and speeches are aimed at confusing them.

Although the Muslims have generally reacted adversely to my views, there is some variety in their positions. Among my critics are some who had opposed the creation of Pakistan. However, the reason why they were opposed to the partitioning of the Indian sub-continent was that they dreamt of converting the whole of India into *Dar-ul-Islam*. Therefore, now that Pakistan has already been created, their efforts are directed towards merging the rest of India with that Islamic state.

On the other hand, there are Indian Muslims who are being modernized gradually. At present, such Muslims are few and they are confused. They have doubts and anxieties about their future, and they are worried about the security of the Muslim community itself in India. Being in doubt and feeling insecure, these Muslims oppose any new and different approach to the communal problem in India. They imagine that the security of Indian Muslims lies in clinging to the traditional structure of Indian society. In short, they believe that if Muslims were to have any place in Indian life they should remain exactly as they are today. Hence even such Muslims are opposed to my views.

Of these two broad types of Indian Muslims who find my views unpalatable, I would not attempt to initiate a dialogue with those who dream of converting India to Islam and of merging it ultimately with Pakistan. If these people believe that it is their duty to convert all Indians to Islam by whatever means they can think of, they are the exact counterpart of those extremist Hindus who similarly wish to liquidate all Indian Muslims even if it involved mass extermination. I come from the Muslim community and yet I cannot entirely blame the extremist Hindu communalists. Whereas the extremist Muslim communalists have aggressive plans to destroy the Hindu community the extremist Hindus, in reaction to them, want to eliminate the Muslims in self-defence. Thus I view extremist Hindu communalism as a reaction to Muslim communalism. Unless Muslim communalism is eliminated, Hindu communalism will not disappear. At the same time, one has to bear in mind that extremist Muslim communalists are so much obsessed by their grand dream of converting the whole of India to Islam that no argument at present will effect any change in their attitude. Their grand dream has to terminate in a grand disillusionment first. They must become aware of the fact that their efforts are foredoomed to failure and their objectives are unat-

tainable. Today, they cannot be made aware of the futility
of their ambition and hence my appealing to them would
serve no useful purpose.

However, I believe it to be my duty to appeal to those
Indian Muslims who are confused and therefore still un-
certain in their approach to the communal problem in
India. They are misguided and, therefore, they are communalist. To initiate a dialogue with them and to make
them aware of an alternative approach to the problem
will be helpful. Wherever I travel in India, I meet local
Muslims and try to discuss the issue with them. I keep
an open mind: for they may have some genuine problems
and difficulties. I try to understand them. Sometimes, I
I succeed; sometimes, I fail. Generally, old and tradition-
bound Muslims uniformly oppose my views. Often, they
boycott my public meetings or have them cancelled. However, the young Muslims I meet at such discussions do
not greet my views with the hostility shown by the older
generation. This does not, however, mean that they
agree with me on all points. But neither do they agree
with their elders. I have always felt that these younger
Muslims are struggling to free themselves from the
shackles of rigid, orthodox thinking. My appeal is addressed
to them.

Even the younger generation of Indian Muslims imagine
that it is the Hindus who are responsible for all their
problems and difficulties. They often ask me why I single
out Muslim communalism for criticism. It is true that
even Hindus are communal-minded. And it is wrong to
say that I have kept silent about Hindu communalism
while criticizing Muslim communalism in India. I have
been ceaselessly criticizing the movement for a ban on
cow-slaughter. However, when I criticize Hindu communalist trends I do not criticize the Hindus as such. Nor is

it the purpose of my criticism to ensure that Muslims
are able to eat beef. That would be a näive way of look-
ing at the problem. My criticism of the movement for a
ban on cow-slaughter is from the agricultural and economic point of view. I believe that such a ban would adversely affect two major national interests: the development
of Indian agriculture and hence of the Indian economy.
Similarly, when I criticize certain Muslim attitudes, I criticize them in the context of broad national interests which
should be the concern of all Indians regardless of their
religious faith. I do not criticize Muslims as such.

It is an old habit of Indian Muslims to blame Hindus
for their woes. However, the Indian Muslim intelligentsia
has never really been critically introspective. It has not
sought to relate its problems to its own attitudes. It has
not developed a self-searching, self-critical attitude. Compared to the Hindus, the Indian Muslims accepted Western education rather late. As a consequence, the Muslims
remained comparatively backward in several fields. The
real cause of Muslim backwardness is found in the Muslim opposition to educational reform during the early days
of British rule in India. Behind this view was a peculiar
sense of resentment. Muslims in India believed that the
British snatched away from their predecessors what was
a Muslim Empire. When Sir Syed Ahmed Khan urged
Muslims to accept modern Western education the *ulema*
of Deoband came out with the *fatwa* that Sir Syed was
a *kafir*. How can one blame the Hindus for this?

Muslims remained backward because they were religion-
bound revivalists who refused to modernize themselves.
Sir Syed Ahmed Khan in this light appears as a great
visionary who heralded the Indian Muslim renaissance.
It was due to his great efforts that the rigidly religious
mind of Indian Muslims began to show the first signs of

a thaw. Educated Muslims began to redefine life in terms of the modern age. They gave up the grand dream of converting India to Islam. This was the beginning of a great upheaval among educated Indian Muslims. A process of transformation had begun. It was this process that should have brought Muslims close to Hindus and broadened their view of man and society. The trend of this process was toward a view according to which Hindus and Muslims would have been looked upon as equals.

This process was, however, ironically reversed because modern Indian Muslims proved unequal to the task. Their modernity proved limited and they lacked the broad vision that could have ensured the complete success of the Aligarh renaissance. Ironically, this very process separated the Muslims from the Hindus instead of bringing them closer together. The old Muslim habit of blaming the Hindus for their problems reappeared and was set more firmly than ever. Although Sir Syed Ahmed Khan was free from the vice of religious fanaticism, he lacked the virtue of being free from the atavistic vanity of an inheritor of the Moghul past. In this very period, when it was possible for a national consciousness to emerge, Sir Syed Ahmed Khan himself succumbed to the egoistic conception that Muslims were the conquerors of India. It was he who was the father of separatist Muslim nationalism, and not Jinnah as it is erroneously supposed. Jinnah is only a later version of Sir Syed, revised and enlarged. Thus the aberrent modern Muslim himself was responsible first for a separatist Muslim nationalism and later for the creation of Pakistan. The foundation of Muslim nationalism is the postulate that Hindu and Muslim societies are autonomous and parallel social structures.

It is no fault of the Hindus that the Indian Muslims embraced this theory of a separate, Muslim nationalism.

Nor is it the fault of the Hindus that Indian Muslims regarded Hindus in Pakistan as hostages ensuring their own (Indian Muslims') security in India. It is only once in a while that an individual or a society gets an opportunity to make or mar its own future. The Muslims lost their rare chance of embracing modernity simultaneously with the Hindus when they yielded to the pressure exerted on them by the *ulema* of Deoband and rejected English education. History gave them another chance a little later— the opportunity to strengthen Indian nationalism by joining forces with the Hindus. But they let go even this opportunity by succumbing to the erroneous notion that Hindu and Muslim societies were autonomous and parallel social structures. They paid scant heed even to geographical realities and refused to consider where they lived and would live in the future. The problems faced by Indian Muslims today can be traced back to these two lost opportunities. If a chance that comes only once in a century is wasted, it takes another century to make up for the loss.

It is high time now that younger Muslims became critically introspective and learnt the nature of their own mistake. It is a tragic fact that there does not yet exist a class of critically introspective young Muslims in India. A society which puts the blame on the Hindus for its own communalism can hardly be called introspective. If Hindu communalism is responsible for Muslim communalism, by the same logic it would follow that Muslim communalism is equally responsible for Hindu communalism. The truth of the matter is that the Muslim intelligentsia has not yet given up its postulate of parallel society. It has still not learnt to separate religion from politics. Their idea of religious freedom is merely that the structure of the Muslim society in India should remain unaltered. Basically, they are still 'Muslim nationalists'. They have not accepted the modern concept of nationalism, and hence their attempts to preserve Muslim nationalist trends in the present structure of the Indian polity. There is a curious collusion between these Indian Muslims and the others who envisage the conversion of India to Islam. This is precisely what brings Maulana Abul Hasan Nadvi of the Jamaat-e-Islami and Dr Faridi of the Majlis-e-Mashawarat together on the same platform.

These are the two broad trends one discerns among Indian Muslims today. One group has taken its inspiration from Shah Waliullah and the other regards Sir Syed Ahmed Khan as its mentor and pioneer. Today it is necessary to reject both. The Hindus too had similar trends; they exist even today. But the Hindus also had a liberal humanist tradition. Nehru kept this tradition alive; Gandhi was a symbol of this same great tradition. That the Indian Muslim community could not produce a Gandhi underscores its failure. Only the North-West Frontier Province could produce a great man like Abdul Ghaffar Khan. But it is significant, though not difficult to understand, that Indian Muslims did not respond to him.

Will the younger generation of Indian Muslims face this challenge? This is their third, and perhaps last, chance to liberate and modernize themselves. If they avail themselves of it, they can still make up for the loss the Muslim community has suffered by wasting the two previous opportunities to create a tradition of modern, enlightened liberalism. The only effective answer to the problems of Indian Muslims would involve on their part a total rejection of the prejudices of history. Only when they rid themselves of the misconceptions that history and tradition produce can they arrive at the conception of a free, modern mind committed only to fundamental human values.

The articles which follow are an attempt in that direction. I would earnestly appeal to my young Muslim readers to give them serious, critical consideration.

I would also like to make a similar request to my Hindu readers. Several Hindu friends have welcomed the attempts of persons like me to modernize the Muslim community in India. However, there is a class of Hindus which views with suspicion any Muslim's attempt to transform the consciousness of his community. This does not surprise me. The motives of even a man of Gandhi's stature were suspiciously viewed by a vast number of Indian Muslims. In such a situation, it is but inevitable that a number of Hindus would suspect the motives of an ordinary man like me. It would scarcely be worth the trouble to try to convince them of my *bona fides*. However, there are some Hindus who view Muslim society as a society which, like any other, can be transformed in the course of time. My appeal is addressed to such Hindus. I urge them to accept the facts of the situation first: there is no class of thoroughly secular Muslims in India today. At the same time the idea of a common Indian nationality requires that Muslim society be integrated in the fabric of a secular Indian society. The only way in which this can be achieved is by first creating a small class of modern, liberal and secular Muslims. This is precisely what people like me are attempting to do. Personally, I believe that no religion can provide the foundation for an ideal society. It follows that neither Islam nor Hinduism can be the basis of an ideal social order. Several people ask me where precisely I differ from communal Hindus. It should be fairly obvious now where I differ from them and how radical the differences are. However, I agree with them on certain points and it would be worthwhile to demarcate clearly the area of agreement between us. I agree with them that Muslim communalism is a strong force in this country at present. I also agree with them that in this nation minorities have a claim to equal rights and equal opportunities but they should not have a claim to special status or privileges. I also agree with them that Kashmir is a part of India and that every Pakistani aggression on Indian soil must be answered by a strong counter-attack. Finally, I agree with the communalist Hindu's view that Pakistan was not the last demand of the Muslims of this sub-continent. Even today, both among Indian Muslims and among the rulers of Pakistan, there are influential groups whose 'last demand' would be the conversion of the whole of India to Islam.

However, I consider suicidal the Hindu communalist attempt to answer Muslim communalism by obscurantist Hindu revivalism. Muslim communalism will be defeated only when the Hindu achieves a greater degree of social progress and modernizes himself. By making the Hindus more obscurantist—by making them more puritan and orthodox—Muslim communalism can never be eliminated. The movement for a ban on cow-slaughter provides an apt example. I oppose the ban on agro-economic grounds. But I oppose it even more strongly on non-economic grounds, because if the Hindu belief in the sacredness of the cow is encouraged, it would prevent the Hindus from modernizing themselves and from achieving a greater degree of social progress. The Hindus have slid backward only because of their religious obscurantism. Mahmud Ghazanvi could defeat Hindu armies simply by using herds of cows as a shield for his own army! One hopes that such history will not be repeated in modern times. Hindus must discard all those religious beliefs which

hindered their progress and deprived them of their freedom. I say this as a friend of the Hindus and not as an
antagonist. No Muslim communalist will object to Hindu
obscurantism for the reasons I give here, simply because
no Muslim communalist ever wishes that Hindu society
should become modern and dynamic. As a matter of fact,
to protect their own mediaeval obscurantist beliefs, the
Muslims would find it convenient that the Hindus also
remained mediaeval-minded religious puritans. I attack
all aspects of mediaeval religious obscurantism whether it
is Muslim or Hindu. And hence I am opposed to the movement for a ban on cow-slaughter. Eighty-five per cent of
the population of this country is Hindu and therefore the
progress of this nation depends on the Hindus becoming
dynamic, modern and advanced. And I want this nation
to be advanced, powerful and prosperous because my
individual future is inextricably tied up with it. I would
go even further and tell the communalist Hindus that they
cannot free Muslims from the shackles of their own
obscurantist beliefs if the Hindus themselves remain reli-
gion-bound. To modernize Indian Muslims, Hindus must
first strengthen the forces of modernization among themselves. When Indian Muslims are shocked out of their
slumber by the advancement and modernization of Hindu
society, a similar process will start in Muslim society and
that would help the efforts of persons like me.

Hindu communalists should not continue to make the
tragic blunder of mistaking every Muslim for a communalist. It is true that today it is difficult to find a thoroughly
secular Muslim in India. But if we want secular-minded
Muslims in the near future, we must encourage and support those Muslims who are already stepping in that direction. One can cite numerous cases where the Hindus can
and ought to support certain Muslims by acknowledging

the worth of their efforts. For example, Mr Sadiq is making sincere and systematic efforts in Kashmir to free Kashmiri Muslims from the hold that Sheikh Abdullah has on their minds. It would also be honest to admit that the Health Minister of Maharashtra, Dr Rafiq Zakaria is making sincere efforts to propagate family planning among Indian Muslims. I mention this particularly because the communalist Hindu, in his zeal to condemn all Muslims as communalists, weakens the emerging liberal and modern forces among the Muslims. Indian Muslims will change only when they begin to present a differentiated picture in their thoughts and their view of society. Hindus would also benefit from such differentiation among the Muslims. For as long as the Muslims remain monolithic in their thinking, their communalism will become increasingly awesome. If they divide into two camps, the modern liberals and the orthodox puritans, their communalism would be much weakened. I suggest that communalist Hindus, and particularly the younger Hindus, should pause and consider this.

History, which has bred prejudices and animosity, is a hindrance to all of us. All of us have to come out of the grip of our prejudices which originate in our past. Hindu communalists must also break away from the grip of their prejudices. It is not the fault of the young Brahmins of today that their ancestors gave inhuman treatment to the untouchables, and today's Indian Muslim is not responsible for the oppression to which Mahmud Ghazanvi or Aurangzeb subjected the Hindus. Fortunately, there is a class of Hindus today which bears the burden of its ancestors' sins and conscientiously tries to undo the damage by embracing social equality as a fundamental value. Similarly, there has to emerge a class of Muslims which would accept the sins of Aurangzeb and, to undo the damage, would therefore embrace the concept of secular citizenship. The emergence and sustained growth of such a class of modern, secular, dynamic liberals is the only effective answer to the Hindu-Muslim communal problem. And therefore, my appeal to communal Hindus is that they should free themselves from historical prejudices before they examine the views expressed by me in the articles that follow.

2

THE CHIEF OBSTACLE IN THE
WAY OF MUSLIM INTERGRATION

The demand for Pakistan was based on the theory that
there was nothing common between the Hindus and the
Muslims of India. In order to justify this demand it was
argued that the presence of a Hindu minority in Pakistan
was a guarantee for the safety of a Muslim minority in
India. In short, a majority of the Muslims demanded in 1947
that (i) an independent sovereign state be established comprising provinces with a Muslim majority, (ii) the Hindus
should remain as a minority in Pakistan, and (iii) the
Hindus in Pakistan should be held as hostages by the
Pakistani Muslims for the well-being of Indian Muslims.
The Hindus reluctantly conceded this demand and thus
the decision to divide the sub-continent was reached.

I consider the Hindu-Muslim problem as a problem
specific to India. Its scope does not extend to the entire
sub-continent, nor is it necessary to extend it in that manner. The Hindu-Muslim problem in the sub-continent
no longer remains an issue between two communities; it
has now assumed the proportions of an international dispute between India and Pakistan. It is therefore a question of international relations. It can be seen as a conflict
between two different kinds of nationalism and the motive

forces operating behind them. We are therefore compelled
to discuss the nature of the decision made in 1947.

To discuss the decision to partition the sub-continent
is to discuss the ambivalence that clouds it. It is necessary
to clarify all the implications of this decision and to discuss the obstacles in the way of its implementation. It is
not only a matter of discussing the decision to partition
the sub-continent. We must also remember that we decided to integrate the rest of India on secular lines in 1947.
Our leaders decided to grant Indian Muslims as well as
all other minorities equal status as citizens of India. We
gave ourselves a Constitution which grants equal opportunities to all citizens and an even more important aspect
of this decision is that we vowed that we would create a
multi-religious, secular, and integrated Indian society. The
moment we made this historic decision, the Hindu-Muslim
problem was in one sense eliminated for two reasons: (i)
we gave Pakistan to the Muslims in order to solve the
Hindu-Muslim problem once for all; and (ii) even more
importantly, we decided to create an integrated nation
based on equal citizenship, cancelled separate electorates,
and abolished special representation. We abolished all
kinds of religious prerogatives. The moment we did this,
we solved the problem for all practical purposes.

Today, the real problem we face in India is that of creating a secular, integrated Indian society. We are concerned
today not with the Hindu-Muslim problem but with that of
removing the obstacles in the way of a liberal society
integrated on secular lines. In short, my theme in this
essay is the problem of Muslim integration in the fabric
of a liberal and secular Indian society.

To discuss this problem certain preconditions must be
fulfilled. We need participants in the discussion who are
self-critical, introspective and capable of thinking in a

secular way. Among Indian Muslims there are very few people who are capable of introspection. Individuals like Mr M. C. Chagla and Professor Habib are exceptional. Among Indian Muslims there is a conspicuous absence of unbiased, self-critical and rational individuals who can discuss this problem fruitfully. This is not entirely the fault of individual Indian Muslims. The capacity for self-criticism, the courage to face facts, the ability to lead the community with a critical awareness of one's own virtues and shortcomings, implies the existence of a level of sophistication in the intelligentsia. The Muslim intelligentsia in India lacks these qualities. Their so-called leaders are usually the leaders of a blind, orthodox, and ill-educated community. Such people do not discuss their own faults; rather, they obdurately cling to their own views. All of them put forward the same arguments in the same tone again and again. When they find faults, the faults are invariably those of other people. They do not have the capacity to understand their own mistakes, and when people who lack this capacity pretend to find solutions for a problem, the solutions are hardly useful. When the wrong kind of people enter the fray, discussion does not lead to any meaningful dialogue. It only leads to further mutual bitterness and further aggravation of tensions already in existence.

When I say that the Muslim mind is incapable of critical introspection, I imply that the Hindu intelligentsia has to a certain extent developed this capacity. One sees that the Hindu intelligentsia sometimes refuses to be swept by emotional appeals. During the recent agitation for a ban on cow-slaughter, one saw several instances which could support this observation. Some Hindu intellectuals have been consistently opposing the demand for a ban on cow-slaughter. It is not necessary here to discuss the grounds on which they oppose the demand. Some oppose it because they believe that such a ban would be incompatible with the secular ideals of Indian society. Others oppose it because they believe that the ban would hinder the economic and agricultural progress of the nation. In short, some members of the Hindu intelligentsia view even a religious agitation such as this from a rational viewpoint.

The differential characteristic of an intellectual is that he always analyses problems rationally. If this criterion were to be applied to the so-called Muslim intellectuals we would be sorely disappointed. It would soon become apparent that the 'Muslim intellectual' is not an intellectual in the real sense of the term. He is merely a Muslim. I would cite two examples in support of my observation.

In 1953, the Bharatiya Vidya Bhavan published an abridged edition of the book *Living Prophets* published originally by Thomas and Thomas. Indian Muslims objected to the book on the ground that it contained some misleading statements about the Prophet Muhammad. However, they did not stop at that. They demanded a ban on the book. In fact, they launched a nation-wide agitation to demand enforcement of the ban. It is significant that there was not a single Muslim intellectual in the country to point out that the agitation had an entirely wrong basis, that other people had a right to express their opinions—even if they were wrong opinions and even if they were opinions about the Prophet. When the holy hair enshrined at Hazratbal was found missing, the same attitude was laid bare. I would have been happy if at that time some Muslim intellectual had the courage to point out that it was wrong to give the hair such great importance, and it was certainly senseless that the whole of the Kashmir administration should be brought to a standstill because of the missing hair. But the unfortunate fact remains that not a single intellectual from among the number of Muslims who style themselves as intellectuals had the courage to speak out openly on this occasion.

A personal experience of mine throws light on a different aspect of this issue. At that time I wanted to express the views which I have stated above. But when I wrote an article on the subject and took it to the editor of a journal, he refused to publish it. In fact, he retorted: "Do you want me to have a Muslim demonstration storming my office?" It is hardly necessary to add that the gentleman was a Hindu. A Hindu is used to playing several roles and he is an expert in assuming different forms on different occasions. I have already referred to Hindu intellectuals and given the due praise. But I must frankly state that there is a kind of Hindu who is always terrified when he thinks of Muslims. This is no doubt a shameful state of affairs. At every critical moment this particular type of Hindu pretends to be more of a Muslim than a Muslim himself, and thwarts the attempts of those who are trying to make the average Muslim less of a fanatic.

The real obstacle in the way of secular integration is the vast gulf that separates the intelligentsia of the two communities. An intellectual minority always helps to shape the rest of society on proper lines. It helps to establish a necessary equilibrium. It leads progressive movements in the society. It effectively fights obstinate revivalists. It continuously accepts fresh ideas and welcomes new values. It examines values on the basis of its own rationality. It is conscious of its own faults and shortcomings before it criticizes the defects of others. An intellectual has the capacity for critical introspection. His approach is dispassionate and analytical. The progress of a society is measured by the existence and size of its intellectual minority.

However, such a class does not come into existence in a society all too easily. It is the product of several complex historical, social, political and other processes. Exposure to such processes helps to create a tolerant attitude which is necessary for the existence of an intellectual minority and its movement. Hindu society has gone through such a process. It has withstood the critical pressures inherent in this process. It has therefore been able to give rise to a class of self-critical, liberal intellectuals. The Muslim community in India has not undergone such a process of transformation. It is just about to enter a phase in which this process begins. That is why I consider it a remote possibility that I shall be able to discuss this problem with Muslim leaders whose arguments are at present predictably obstinate.

I do not, however, mean that there are no rational individuals among the Indian Muslims. There are a few exceptional individuals who can think dispassionately and in a secular manner. They are examples of a progressive Muslim mind, but a handful of such people do not make a liberal intellectual class and it is not possible for isolated individuals to have any appreciable effect on society. These people cannot create a movement in the Indian Muslim community because they do not have a place in the community. The moment they became liberals they lost the confidence of their backward and orthodox commuity. Hindu liberals have been far more fortunate. Nehru is an example. In 1946, when anti-Muslim riots erupted in the State of Bihar, Nehru threatened to bomb the rioting Hindus if they would not stop their violence; and yet the Hindus continued to accept Nehru as their leader. In spite of partition, Nehru gave this nation a secular constitution; he gave Muslims equal rights; and yet a large majority of Hindus accepted him as their leader. One can cite numerous examples of this sort. Mr Nirad C. Chaudhury is another example. In his book *The Continent of Circe*, Mr Chaudhury has discussed what he considers the decadence of the Hindu mind. He has attacked the Hindus by calling them degenerate and yet Hindus consider him one of themselves. But the situation with the Muslims is different. Maulana Azad opposed Pakistan and it would be interesting to recall how he was greeted by the Muslims for that. This was twenty years ago. What status has Mr Chagla today in the Indian Muslim community? We know what storm of criticism he had to brave when he proposed the Aligarh University Bill. As long as such a vital difference exists between the mental make-ups of the two communities, Hindu-Muslim tensions are not likely to abate. I think this difference between the two communities is in the nature of a disparity of cultural levels. The wide cultural gulf that separates the two must be bridged. Compared to the Hindus, the Muslims today are culturally backward. They ought to be brought on a level with the Hindus. This would imply the creation of a liberal class in the Muslim community. The Indian Muslims today need, most urgently, a liberal movement.

I do not think that a fruitful discussion of this subject between Hindu and Muslim leaders and intellectuals is going to be possible for another decade or two. Then there will be a meaningful dialogue between the two communities. And when this happens Indian Muslims will have already found an equilibrium. I do visualize the creation, in the near future, of a class of liberals among Indian Muslims. I am not saying this simply because I am an optimist. I feel that after about twenty years Indian Muslims will have the benefit of a new leadership. Such a leadership will not talk of protecting the 'religious' interests of Muslims. It would be a leadership leading different classes and strata of Indian society as a whole.

I shall give only one example of the kind of leadership I have in view, the example provided by Mr George Fernandez. Mr George Fernandez is a Catholic by faith but his faith does not intrude into his social and political life. He is a leader of the working class. He talks not of defending 'Catholic' interests but rather of defending the interests of the working class. People may assess Mr Fernandez's political work in different ways, what is relevant here is the fact that he does not represent the 'religious' interests of Catholics when he speaks as a social and political leader. When he speaks of removing English as the medium of administrative and public communication, he forgets that he is a Catholic. He did not attend the Eucharistic Congress held in Bombay. It is irrelevant whether or not in his personal life he is religious. What is important is the fact that he does not bring his religious interests into public life. I hope that in future Indian Muslims too will have such a leadership. Today they do not have it. In fact, even those Muslim leaders who call themselves Marxists pollute public life with religious interests. Mr Mohammad Iliyas, a Right Communist leader of West Bengal, is a case in point. He styles himself as a working class leader. However, in 1967 he led a demonstration of Muslim devotees seeking to assert their right to offer prayers at a place the ownership of which was in dispute. He led this demonstration on a Friday—the day on which Muslims offer mass prayers. It is important to remember that Mr Iliyas did not pause to consider that dispute about the ownership of the place was *sub judice*. In order to justify his action Mr Iliyas, who had no patience to wait for the verdict of a court of law, made the curious claim that he was defending religious freedom and was therefore defending the fundamental rights of aggrieved citizens. But

surely, Mr Iliyas's 'Marxism', which defines religious freedom as the right to trespass on disputed property even as
a court of law is about to settle the dispute, is an odd
kind of Marxism?

3

READING THE MIND OF
INDIAN MUSLIMS

The previous article was a brief review of the problem of Indian Muslims and its solution. I have described the symptoms of a disease and outlined its treatment without naming the disease as such. One of the reasons for doing so was to focus attention on certain aspects of the problem at the very outset. I also wanted to show how certain pitfalls cannot be avoided when one begins to discuss a problem from the end to the beginning. My main reason, however, was to invite my Muslim friends to do some necessary critical introspection so that they might start the discussion in a frank and systematic manner.

It is my experience that the arguments of Muslim leaders always sound like the arguments of defence attorneys in a court of law. In a court of law the lawyer's sole interest is to win his case. The argument is addressed to a judge, who is a third party and who gives his verdict in the end. If a lawyer defending an alleged murderer argues the defendant's case effectively, his client is acquitted even if he in fact is a murderer. The sole emphasis in this kind of argument is on convincing the judge. Muslim leaders in India argue much in the same manner. One does not know whether they expect some judge to give a favourable verdict in the end. For instance, most Muslim leaders in India advance the odd argument that Muslims were not responsible for partition, and even argue that Hindus alone were responsible for it. Of course, there can be different arguments as to who really was more responsible for partition, but it is factually wrong to suggest that Muslims were not responsible for partitioning the sub-continent. When Muslims say this, they do not want to claim merely that they were not responsible for partition. Their claim is much larger; they want to claim that it was not the Muslims who demanded the partitioning of the sub-continent.

History provides some clues to the strange behaviour and arguments of Indian Muslim leaders. Indian Muslims always tried to impose their own demands on Hindus with the help of the British, who were a third party in the position of a judge. It was enough for the Muslims to have presented effective arguments to the British. If one recalls the entire history of the efforts made to solve the Hindu-Muslim problem, one can easily verify this. It was Muslim leaders who obstinately held that the Hindus should not be granted freedom unless Muslim demands were met. When they saw that the judgment in this dispute was to be given by a third party, they tried to tilt the balance in their own favour even by resorting to an unscrupulous and fallacious argument, and the Hindus who were eager for independence conceded their demand. It is not important to discuss how the third party arrived at its verdict. The important thing is to remember the historical fact that the Muslims got their verdict from a third party. They never even paused to consider that the real decision was to be taken by the Muslims themselves in collaboration with the Hindu majority. They looked at the dispute as if it was a matter of litigation and could never think of the possibility of a compromise.

In short, Indian Muslims committed the most grievous sin of obstructing the movement for Indian independence. They took undue advantage of the presence of a third party. They refused to arrive at a compromise with the Hindus. Muslims in the entire sub-continent were responsible for this. But there is an important difference between Indian and Pakistani Muslims. Muslims in Pakistan did not have to face the consequences of this wrong-headed agitation. In fact, if the agitation were to succeed, it would be of benefit to them. And therefore, it must be said that Pakistani Muslims deliberately took a wrong step, the consequences of which were to be suffered by Muslims who were to remain in India.

But Indian Muslims have committed an even worse sin. They not only relied on a third party but also participated in a movement which aimed at creating a separate nation comprising all provinces which had a Muslim majority. In short, in order to solve their own problems, Indian Muslims as a whole came to an understanding with the British as well as with the Muslim majority provinces; and they refused to make any compromise with Hindus.

What was the nature of this understanding? To solve our problems, argued the Muslims in the sub-continent, a sovereign and independent state comprising provinces with a Muslim majority had to be created. In this new state Hindus should be in a minority. That way only, they further argued, would Muslims in India have security. This argument is known as the hostage theory. In the middle ages the cruel and inhuman practice of holding human beings as hostages was quite common. It is tragic that Muslims in the sub-continent resorted to this old practice to solve their problem.

But the interesting thing is that while Pakistan needed

some Hindus at least as hostages, she did not even keep a sizeable number of them in her territory though the subcontinent was partitioned only because Muslims decided to experiment with the theory of hostages. At that time, several observers had warned that this theory would create a problem of minorities in both India and Pakistan and that in both countries politics would be centered on vengeance wreaked on the minorities. A prominent Muslim intellectual had issued this warning in a book published before partition. Shaukatulla Ansari, at present Governor of Orissa, in his *Pakistan—A Problem of India* published in 1944, has made a very significant observation. He predicted that if the sub-continent were to be partitioned, it would be partitioned in an atmosphere of bitter hostility which would last for generations and would be difficult to eliminate. All of us are witness to the accuracy of his prophecy.

Muslims in India agreed to remain in India as hostages in accordance with the theory propounded by the Muslim League. Why should Indian Muslims complain about it now? Do they say now that this entire theory was wrong? No; their only complaint is that Hindus have started implementing the theory. They are not worrried whether Hindus are themselves unhappy about the theory. Their only demand is that the theory should not affect themselves. All Muslim leaders, following the theory, demand that there should be no anti-Muslim riots in India. If one asked them any question about the fate of Hindus in Pakistan, they would dismiss it. I have already observed that among Indian Muslims there still is no liberal class whose members would take an honest and just view of things. It is sufficient for Muslim leaders in India to argue that Hindus in Pakistan are not treated in an unjust manner. If one points to instances of injustice done to Hindus in

M-4

Pakistan, Indian Muslim leaders have a ready answer. They would say that it is a problem of Pakistan with which they are hardly concerned. On the other hand, they would criticize the questioner for raising an issue which has to do with Pakistan and not with themselves.

The question which arises here is : Why do Indian Muslims make the obviously false claim that Pakistani Hindus are treated with due justice? And why did Indian Muslims earlier refuse to rely on the conscience of Hindus to get full justice for themselves? I shall begin with the first question. Those who claim that Hindus in Pakistan get due justice assume that this entire problem is still a case pending trial in a court. They still imagine, perhaps quite honestly but no doubt unrealistically, that if they argue forcefully enough there still is a third party to give them a verdict in their favour. They do not see the plain fact that the third party has already left the sub-continent and that, in India, it is replaced by the defendant in the case. Now the judge's position is occupied by Hindus. If it is justice that the Indian Muslims expect, they have to win the confidence and goodwill of the Hindu majority. Do these Muslim leaders honestly believe that arguments like those of lawyers in a court of law are going to secure justice for them? But they refuse to look at this problem in a sober and realistic manner. For they still believe that a third party is going to judge their case and that all they need to win their case is an effective argument, however fallacious it may be, coupled with the right amount of pressure. They do not clearly name who the third party in the judge's position is today. But one need not go very deep to find out what is fairly obvious: Indian Muslim leaders believe that in their dispute with the majority in India, Pakistan is the third party occupying the position of the judge.

I must say that the leaders who think so are still living in the pre-Independence age. Some months ago, I had an opportunity of meeting Dr A. J. Faridi, leader of the Majlis-e-Mashawarat. Dr Faridi claims to have a balanced view of things. He also believes that one ought to point out the mistakes committed by Indian Muslims. But it is an interesting experience to discuss this issue with Dr Faridi. Once one enters into an argument with him, Dr Faridi has the knack of evading the very principles he himself professes. For example, when I asked him why Hindus were driven out of West Pakistan, Dr Faridi came up with the fantastic answer that if Vallabhbhai Patel had not sent planes to bring them back the West Pakistani Hindus would not have come back to India at all. In short, Dr Faridi is against any injustice done to anyone. In that respect he is a perfect secularist. But if one chooses to go into factual details about the injustice done to Pakistani Hindus, Dr Faridi would categorically assert that there had never been any act of injustice towards them. On top of this, Dr Faridi is always ready to declare that he would protest the moment he learns that there has been any injustice done to Hindus in Pakistan. However, Dr Faridi always insists on being 'convinced' and, as one might guess, it is very difficult to convince Dr Faridi.

Let us now consider some of the views of Mr Mohammad Ismail, President of the All-India Muslim League. In an interview given to U.N.I. before the last general elections, Mr Mohammad Ismail said, "If I am convinced that the Hindus of Pakistan are ill-treated or that they are forcibly converted to Islam, I would not hesitate to criticize Pakistan. For Islam does not permit such injustice." In short, Mr Mohammad Ismail is always prepared to say that if Pakistan ever treated her Hindus badly he would consider it to be a very wrong thing. The real question

therefore is of determining empirically whether Pakistan
really does so. It is a question of assessing plain facts. It
is the responsibility of whoever argues with Mr Mohammad
Ismail to convince him that it is a fact that Pakistan treats
her Hindus unjustly. Once he is able to convince Mr
Mohammad Ismail about the truth of this proposition, the
rest follows quite easily. As soon as he is convinced, one
would find Mr Mohammad Ismail unsheathing his sword
and brandishing it against Pakistan. But wait! Nothing of
this sort is really going to happen. For even if Pakistan
does in fact treat her Hindu population badly, to convince
Mr Mohammad Ismail of it is not an easy job. In fact, Mr
Mohammad Ismail has decided not to be convinced on
this point by anyone.

When Mr Sri Prakasa was Indian High Commissioner in
Pakistan he had a very significant experience at Karachi.
In his book *Birth of Pakistan,* Mr Sri Prakash has noted
the following incident: In one place a Hindu temple was
broken into. Mr Sri Prakasa brought this to the notice of
a Central Minister of Pakistan. He urged the Minister to
give police protection to the temple. But the Minister refused to do so. What he said is quite memorable. He said,
"Islam has given us the notion of perfect justice. How, in
the circumstances, can a temple be broken into at all?
Such a thing is unthinkable in an Islamic state."!

Mr Sri Prakasa was obviously flabbergasted. It was a
fact that the temple was broken into, but an Islamic state
is always perfectly just. And all Muslim leaders would
readily point to the idea of justice in Islam whenever such
allegations are made. They do not find it necessary to go
into the facts of the matter. If there is any injustice done
to the Hindus in Pakistan, it would be a verifiable proposition. But if facts are different from the claims to perfect
justice made by an Islamic state, not to admit facts is the

way of 'Islamic justice'. Muslims do not use the criteria used for verifying facts by ordinary people. When they do injustice, they apply the canons of 'Islamic justice'. When injustice is done to themselves, they would demand justice by universally accepted principles and would demand an application of the universal criteria of evidence. As to themselves, since Koranic justice is supposed to be equitably applied in an Islamic state, Muslim leaders believe that an Islamic state is always just. It is only others who err. Therefore, outside the Islamic state, Muslim leaders insist on the universally accepted principles of evidence and inference. Such are the double standards they apply.

Can Pakistan ever hope to get a better lawyer than Mr Mohammad Ismail? However, Mr Mohammad Ismail would never admit that he pleads on behalf of Pakistan. Perhaps it does not even occur to him. There are a number of similar examples. When questioned, these Muslim leaders indignantly claim that they are one hundred per cent Indian, that they have fully indentified themselves with the aspirations of this nation, and that they regard the Hindu majority in India as their fellow-citizens. What, however, can one make of these claims when they are seen in juxtaposition with the actual behaviour of Muslim leaders and the opinions they frequently express? Even while they claim to be perfect nationalists, Muslim leaders advance arguments to support the Pakistani claim on Kashmir. In the same way, they argue that all Pakistani infiltrators in Assam are in fact Indian Muslims. It follows that they do not believe in any rules to determine citizenship. They are prepared to go to any absurd length to argue that Pakistani infiltrators are in fact Indians. At the same time, they admit that all Pakistani infiltrators should, on principle, be evicted from India. They claim that they have no quarrel with Hindus as such; and yet, at the same time they issue religious rescripts objecting to the recitation of the Koran after Nehru's death on the ground that such a recitation is not permitted by the side of the dead body of a *kafir*. They want Dr Zakir Husain to be the President of India. However, they are quick to point out that it is unbecoming of a good Muslim to take the oath of office in Hindi or to obtain a benediction from the Shankaracharya. While justifying the creation of Pakistan, they would also argue that they have nothing to do with Pakistan which is a foreign country like any other. They compete with one another to vouch for the peaceful intentions of Pakistan. Who is responsible for disturbing the peace in the sub-continent? Their answer is ready: it is the mistakes of the Indian leadership that have created all the trouble that exists in the sub-continent. Indian leaders, according to these Muslims, have never been reconciled to the creation of Pakistan and hence they bear animosity towards that country. Pakistan quarrels with India over Kashmir. Once Kashmir is handed over to Pakistan, these people argue, there would be no quarrel. It is obvious, they feel, that India has created hostility with Pakistan by not giving up Kashmir.

I would like to point out that these views extend to even further extremes. There is an organisation of Indian Muslims known as the Jamaat-e-Islami. The objective of this organisation is to establish an Islamic State in India. *Margdeep*, the Marathi organ of the party once wrote, "Religious conflicts in India are not likely to be resolved easily. Only when all Indians embrace a single religion, religious conflicts in India would end."

If one tries to view the inconsistencies in the views of Muslim leaders quoted earlier in the light of the above quotation from *Margdeep*, it will be obvious that Muslim leaders are engaged in a gigantic *jehad*—a holy war—against Hindus. This war would be over only when all Indians have embraced Islam. To achieve this objective, Muslim leaders are prepared to indulge in all kinds of acrobatics. It is quite true that they regard themselves as Indians. For they look forward to ruling the entire nation.

Why did Muslims demand Pakistan? The answer is obvious. Muslims believe that their community is a separate nation. Why did they follow Jinnah? This too is obvious. Jinnah's anti-Hindu views attracted them. In this context, one ought to remember that as long as Jinnah had not propounded his two nation theory Muslims did not accept him as their leader. The reasons for all this are quite clear. Muslims were fiercely anti-Hindu. As soon as Jinnah inflamed their communal passions, Muslims supported him. The passion proved to be so consuming that Indian Muslims failed to see its simple consequence which would turn them into a minority everywhere in India.

However, it must be pointed out that the support of Indian Muslims to the creation of Pakistan was not entirely based on emotional frenzy. It was also based on the theory of hostages. At the same time, Indian Muslims believed that India would eventually be ruled by Islam. The creation of Pakistan was only the first step towards an integrated Islamic state in India. One has only to recall Jinnah's tactics for the creation of Pakistan to see this point. He tried to induce the princely States in Rajasthan to join Pakistan. He tried to get Junagadh merged with Pakistan. He instigated Hyderabad to rebel against India. His propaganda that riots took place in India alone disregarded its consequence in Pakistan itself. What did the Muslims expect? They expected Hyderabad to become independent. They expected Bhopal to follow. Junagadh had already joined Pakistan. Kashmir had a Muslim majority and would there-

fore naturally go to Pakistan. They expected all princely
States to refuse to join India and to proclaim their own
independence. They predicted balkanization of India, from
which Muslims would eventually benefit. These hopes were
later proved to have been false. Sardar Patel merged the
princely States within the Indian Union and thus shattered
their hopes. This is why Muslim leaders hate Sardar Patel.
One can easily understand why Dr Faridi insists that it
was Patel who brought Hindus from Pakistan to India.

In my opinion, Muslim society still mentally lives in the
pre-partition world. I would like to cite another personal
experience. Sometime ago, I visited Agra where I met a
few educated Muslim youths. I asked them only one
question: "Today you complain that Hindus are suspici-
ous of you. I think this is an inevitable consequence of
the creation of Pakistan. Why did the educated Indian
Muslims in India fail to see the terrible consequences of
partition?" These young men came up with a significant
answer. They said: "We would have remained a permanent minority in India. A nation is goverened by the whims
of the majority. We would have been utterly helpless."
In fact, Indian Muslims are even today a minority. If any
thing, they are a much smaller minority now than before
partition. But when Indian Muslims express the views mentioned above, they believe that they have freed themselves
from Hindu domination. One can understand such views
if they are expressed by Pakistani Muslims. However, one
finds that views which might be expected to be voiced by
Pakistani Muslims are in fact voiced by Indian Muslims.
The reason is painfully obvious. Indian Muslims still regard themselves as Pakistanis, and they believe that their
emancipation has been ensured by the creation of Pakistan.
They expect Pakistan to deliver them fully someday. And
therefore they indulge in fallacious and hypocritical argu-

ments. Those who cannot resort to such arguments simply blame the Hindus for injustice done to themselves.

In sum, Muslims cannot reconcile themselves with the nationalism of any country where they are in a minority. They wanted Pakistan because they feared to remain a permanent minority, and they also knew that the creation of Pakistan would not solve the problem of Muslims in this sub-continent. A Muslim periodical recently observed that while partition had solved the problem of some Indian Muslims, the problem of other Indian Muslims was yet to be solved. Mr Suhrawardy said in a speech after partition that partition had solved the problem only of Muslims in Pakistan. It was necessary, he said, to tackle the problem of Indian Muslims. And a little before this, he had observed in a public meeting in Calcutta, "Is Pakistan our last demand? I will not try to answer this question; but I can say, that is our latest demand." Each time the latest demand would be a new one. One might ask, "Which is the last demand?" It is obvious that the last demand would be the whole of India. Today, the latest demand is Kashmir. The next demand is going to be Assam and then for a corridor to link the two wings of Pakistan. I hope my readers are familiar with Mr Bhutto's views in this direction. Those Indian Muslim leaders who loudly proclaim that they have nothing to do with Pakistan should have assailed Mr Bhutto. However, it is significant that none of them uttered so much as a word of protest against Mr Bhutto' statements.

What, according to the Muslims, is the solution to the problem of Muslims in India? It seems that the only solution which occurs to them is the establishment of an Islamic state in India. The Jamaat-e-Islami has already a programme to achieve this objective. And what if they fail to achive it? Then they would seek to establish within the sovereign state of India a sovereign Islamic society. This idea of a state within a state, and a society within a society, appeals to them. One has only to take a look at the nine-point programme of the Majlis-e-Mashawarat to know this. The Mashawarat has demanded that the Indian Parliament should have no power to legislate in matters concerning Indian Muslims. Salahuddin Oweisi, a member of the Andhra Pradesh Legislative Assembly, has in fact publicly suggested, "There should be a separate Muslim state within each state of India."

4

MUSLIMS : THE SO-CALLED
NATIONALISTS AND THE COMMUNALISTS

All Muslim leaders unanimously complain that injustice
is done to Muslims in India. However, they have a strange
definition of injustice. They suggest, indirectly no doubt,
that the very fact that India has a Hindu majority is itself
a great injustice to Muslims. How else can one understand
the programme of the Mashawarat which demands sovereign rights for the Muslim community? In their own way
Muslim leaders are continuously trying to remove this injustice. One of the methods of ensuring justice is to claim
that Pakistani infiltrators in Assam are not Pakistani at all.
A second method is to demand the granting of Indian
citizenship to those Pakistanis who are illegal residents of
Bihar, West Bengal and some other States of India. A
third method is to oppose family planning. A professor
from Aligarh University was quite frank about this. He
said: "Hindus cannot keep us permanently in a minority.
Remember the history of Canada. How did the question
of Quebec arise? Those citizens of Quebec who are of
English origin are Protestants who practise family planning. But those who are of French origin are Catholics
who never planned their families nor are doing
so even today. As a result, the number of French-

speaking Catholics in Quebec has increased in relation to
the number of English-speaking Protestants. Now the
French-speaking Catholics have started protecting their
own rights and interests. We shall follow the same example. If not today, fifty years hence; if not fifty, a hundred
years hence. This country will eventually be swept by an
Islamic tide". The professor was quite forthright in expres-
sing his views. There are others, leaders of Indian Muslims,
who say the same thing although they couch it in clever
phrases. They say, "Our religion does not permit family
planning. Grant us the freedom to practise our religion."

The Urdu viewspaper *Radiance* commenting on the
report of the last census in India, said, "In the last ten
years the Muslim population in India has increased by
4 per cent more than the Hindus. Therefore, Muslims need
not despair about their future."

It would be wrong to dismiss the examples I have cited
above as the stray opinions of a handful of individuals.
I have been moving throughout India for the last few
months. I have been meeting Muslims from various strata
of society. Nine out of every ten people I have met hold
similar views. Some of them go to even further extremes.
To counter my arguments, some people have asked me,
"We were the rulers of this country. Do you want us now
to become slaves?" When I asked them what they proposed
to do they came up with the following answer: "Fight
the Hindus. We are still capable of fighting!" "Then why
don't you?", I asked them. "Give us your support! If all
Muslims unite we can easily defeat the Hindus. With their
unflinching faith Muslims can defeat even the most
formidable enemy. This is the lesson of Islam. Please
remember the battle of Badr!"

It may be useful to understand the allusion to the battle
of Badr. The battle of Badr was the first fought by Mus-

lims. It was a battle in which the Prophet scored a victory over his opponents. His army was badly outnumbered. It consisted of 310 faithful Muslims. His antagonists were the army of the Quraish tribe of Mecca. It numbered more than a thousand. Various explanations of the success of the Prophet's army can be offered. However, that he was victorious is a historical fact and so this battle occupies the position of a memorable turning point in the history of Islam and according to Muslims, in the history of the whole world! The Muslim mind is still under the spell of this historical victory. When we discuss defeats and victories in battles, we resort to the scientific method. We explain the clashes between, for instance, Babar and Rana Sang or Abdally and the Marathas in a scientific manner. A scientific explanation of Babar's victory would be based on the fact that his guns were superior to the weapons used by his adversary. While explaining the outcome of the battle fought between Abdally and the Marathas at Panipat, one would refer to a certain battle-formation at Panipat which was decisive in determining the course of the fight. One can point out that all the three major battles fought at Panipat fall into a single pattern. The victorious side in each of them was placed in a certain advantageous position on the battlefield. There is a hill formation on the Panipat plain which has always proved advantageous to the army which could occupy it. A military expert has commented that the Marathas made a mistake in occupying a disadvantageous position on the battlefield. This would be regarded as a scientific explanation. However, the Muslim mind is averse to accepting scientific explanations. It sees in every Islamic victory a repetition of the battle of Badr. Why did Abdally win? The answer is that he was a Muslim. Why did the Marathas lose? The answer is that they were *kafirs*. How could a handful of Muslims win? The answer is that they were faithful. Why then did the Arabs suffer a crushing defeat at the hands of the Israelis? The answer, this time, is that Arab leaders were not faithful Muslims! The Arabs were led by Nasser. What exactly do these Muslims mean when they criticize Nasser for lack of faith in Islam? The answer, again, is obvious: Nasser is unfaithful because he refuses to bring about the rule of the *Shariat* in Egypt. How could a handful of Muslims rule India for a thousand years? It is simple: they were possessed by a tremendous religious zeal. How can Muslims regain their lost power in India? To this the answer is again very obvious : Muslims in India have to be made more devout!

Leaders like Dr Syed Mahmud of the Majlis-e-Mashawarat believe that Muslim rule in India is essential not only for the benefit of Indian Muslims but for the benefit of all Indians. Once upon a time, Dr Syed Mahmud used to be a leader of the Congress party. In other words, he is one of those people who are described as 'Nationalist Muslims'. For the last several years this dubious type called 'Nationalist Muslim' has been active in our national life. At one time, when I had very naïve notions about politics, I used to view a 'Nationalist Muslim' with great respect. The time has now come for me to confess my earlier blunder. I have seen him at close quarters during recent years. Today I know that the 'Nationalist Muslim' is a strange animal having neither head nor tail; however he is an animal of doubtful pedigree who can be quite dangerous. I no more take a 'Nationalist Muslim' at his face value.

Dr Syed Mahmud is a 'Nationalist Muslim'. I met him at Delhi. When I asked him why he thought it fit to establish an organisation like the Majlis-e-Mashawarat and why he wanted to have a separate platform for the Muslims, his answer appeared to be very sober. He said:

"There are riots. After the riots Muslims protest against them. But nothing happens. These riots ought to stop. Muslims must feel secure. They must feel that they too have a role to play in our national life. This is why we established the Majlis". No sane person would disagree with Dr Mahmud on these points. At the most, one may wonder whether it is necessary to have a separate platform comprising Muslims alone to achieve this objective. But Dr Syed Mahmud did not stop at that. He continued, "And as you know, the situation in this country is deteriorating day by day. *It is quite well-known that Hindus are incapable of ruling a country. This is what history has proved adequately. We are going down the drain as a nation because Muslims in this country have no share in power. Muslims should develop initiative and participate in the government of this nation. Only Muslims can save this nation from doom."* (Emphasis added) From these remarks it should be obvious to anyone how deep is the concern of Dr Syed Mahmud for the future of this nation. To reform it Muslims ought to take their share in ruling this nation. This is the firm belief of Dr Syed Mahmud. He believes that history has proved the inability of Hindus to rule.

We may next turn to the comments made by Mr Khalil-ullah Husaini, Chief of Tamir-e-Millat in *Irshad*, the organ of the Jamaat-e-Islami following the Chinese aggression of 1962: "This defeat has proved that our present rulers have no capacity to rule! The only alternative this nation has is to hand over all power to those who ruled this country for one thousand years!"*

Is there any difference between the views of Dr Syed Mahmud and the leaders of Jamaat-e-Islami? I, for one, find none; and yet Dr Syed Mahmud is regarded as a

* *Irshad*, November 1963

nationalist. We must all examine our own concept of nationalism to find out what kind of people it can really accommodate. Is the aspiration of a minority to rule the majority to be regarded as nationalistic? Or is one to regard nationalism as an advocacy of national interests based on contemporary concepts of fundamental ethical values embodying humanism and secular justice? Those who regard these so-called Muslims as nationalists have to answer these questions.

These nationalist Muslims are often loudly congratulated for having opposed the creation of Pakistan. In order to know where exactly they stand, we ought to take a look at the precise nature of the differences between nationalist Muslims and the Muslim League. The Muslim League held that Muslims in this country must enjoy a privileged and special position in the government. Initially, Jinnah advocated the same views. In short, the Muslim League believed that the current of nationalism in this country contained a separate sub-current of Muslim sub-nationalism! Jinnah wanted this sub-nationalism to be recognised and enshrined in the Constitution itself by granting the Muslims greater representation than their population would entitle them. Nehru opposed the very idea of such sub-nationalism. He refused to concede special representation to Muslims. The real conflict was thus between these two positions. Jinnah's position was that Indian nationalism should make a compromise with Muslim nationalism. Nehru's position was that such separatist sub-nationalism should be rejected on principle. This was not a political issue at all. While Jinnah represented the Muslim movement of a separate, religion-based nationalism, Nehru refused to accept such a concept of nationalism. This was the basis of the conflict that led to the creation of Pakistan. Neither the Muslims nor Jinnah quarreled with

Hindu leaders such as Savarkar or Golwalkar. On the contrary, it seems that Jinnah was basically in agreement with Savarkar. At the annual session of the Hindu Maha Sabha at Ahmedabad, Savarkar referred in his presidential address to Muslim nationalism by saying, "It appears that there exists a separate Muslim nation within India." This must be considered significant in the above context. Savarkar admitted the existence of a separate Muslim nationalism. He had even shown his willingness to give them a written guarantee that their culture, their language, and their proportional representation would be safeguarded. The only thing Savarkar denied to the Muslims was a separate, independent and sovereign state. In this regard, it must be noted that only Nehru held a secular Indian nationalist position. He believed in secular integration in the strictest sense of the term. Jinnah did not want secular integration. He wanted various sub-nationalist currents to exist within the stream of Indian nationalism. Moreover, he wanted to keep special privileges for the sub-nations. When Nehru refused to grant such special privileges, Jinnah demanded Pakistan. We must remember these historical facts in this context.

In this connection, it is often argued that the Congress committed a great blunder by refusing to give the Muslim League one-third of the total seats in the Uttar Pradesh Cabinet of 1937. Those who argued so probably believed that this was merely a political strategy. I would urge that it is necessary to view both the Congress and the Muslim League from a non-political point of view. The demands of Muslim leaders were based on religion. This was not, therefore, merely a question of granting a few seats more to the Muslim League. At that time Jinnah said that the Muslims wanted to share power with the Hindus. The idea was to secure a fifty per cent share of power for the Muslims. When this attempt failed, the Muslims demanded an independent sovereign state of their own.

What would have happened if there were a compromise according to the demands of the Muslim League in 1937? This would have meant a recognition of Muslims as a separate entity by the Constitution. The Muslims would have thus acquired a special position and special privileges. This would have created a perpetual controversy about the privileges. Muslim leaders, however, would have interpreted these privileges in quite a different manner. They could have, and probably would have, vetoed any proposed Bill affecting Muslim interests, and this would have affected the very progress of the nation. Within a single state, the two nationalisms would have clashed continuously. There would have been a terrible civil war. The conflict we witness today between India and Pakistan would have then assumed the form of a civil war within the sub-continental state of India.

I should not be misunderstood as a person indirectly justifying the creation of Pakistan by pointing to the possibility of a civil war. It is not a question merely of a civil war. In the course of history, many nations have had to face a civil war for the sake of preserving their integrity as nations. Sometimes, it is necessary to take such a risk. It is necessary in many instances to suppress separatist tendencies most ruthlessly. The question here is how we would have faced this challenge. Would we have ruthlessly crushed a rebellion? The only honest answer to this question would be in the negative. For in an undivided India a specially privileged Muslim community would have vigorously continued a movement for the Islamicization of India. In such a situation, it is most likely that the Muslim League and the so-called 'Nationalist Muslims' would have joined forces.

This strategy of 'Nationalist Muslim' leaders is amply suggested by their own speeches during the period in question. During those days, Maulana Hussain Ahmad Madni was considered a great 'Nationalist Muslim' leader. He was President of the Jamiat-e-Ulema-i-Hind. When the *ulema* convened a conference in Delhi in the year 1945, he said in his presidential address, "It is the non-Muslims who are the field of action for this 'tabligh' of Islam and form the raw material for this splendid activity..... we are opposed to the idea of limiting the right of missionary activities of Islam within any particular area. The Muslims have got a right in all the nooks and corners of India by virtue of the great struggle and grand sacrifices of their ancestors in this country. Now it is our duty to maintain that claim and try to widen its scope, instead of giving it up."*

The same learned Maulana has said elsewhere, "If Dara had triumphed, Muslims would have stayed in India but not Islam. Since Aurangzeb triumphed, both Muslims and Islam were here to stay."! According to the Maulana, the faith Dara followed was not genuine Islam because Dara wanted to tolerate the Hindus. He did not insist on the rule of the *Shariat*. He did not interpret religion 'correctly', that is, in strict accordance with the tradition. From the above views of the Maulana it should be clear what kind of Islam a majority of 'Nationalist Muslims' subscribed to and what, in the final analysis, their great goals were.

What was the difference between Jinnah and the nationalist Muslims? While Jinnah wanted a separate state, the nationalist Muslims wanted the whole of India. Jinnah

* *The Deoband School and the Demand for Pakistan* by Z. H. Faruqi, Asia Publishing House, Bombay, 1963, p. 117.

knew that it was impossible to get the whole of India, and therefore he settled for Pakistan. Many nationalist Muslims believe that a *jehad* against the Hindus would have got a much larger reward. That is why they opposed the creation of Pakistan. Dr Munje, a leader of the Hindu Mahasabha, once said, "This Jinnah appears to be a fool. He can swallow up the whole of India. I do not understand why he is demanding a separate state."! I am certain that when he said this, Dr Munje had the religious motives of Indian Muslims in mind.

Muslim leaders always blame Hindu communalism for the partition. I fail to see where, in this entire discussion, Hindu communalism comes in. The clash was between Nehru and Jinnah, and Gandhi and Jinnah; Savarkar and Golwalkar are not in the picture at all. Jinnah was not fighting Savarkar and Golwalkar. He never mentioned their communalism. Jinnah accused Gandhi of being a Hindu communalist, refusing to concede his demands. He criticized Nehru in the same way. Similarly, when Muslim leaders hold communalists responsible for the partition, they want to suggest that it was Gandhi and Nehru who were 'Hindu communalists.' The implications are clear: they charge every Hindu with being a communalist. At the same time, they make the strange claim that every Muslim is a nationalist.

The real conflict, therefore, was not between Hindu and Muslim communalists. It was a conflict between the secular nationalism of Gandhi and Nehru and the religious nationalism of Indian Muslims. It is true that Gandhi and Nehru failed to keep the country undivided through secular integration. But this failure is not theirs alone. It is the collective failure of all of us. The stark reality is that Hindu society does not have the strength and capacity to accept this challenge. This painful reality was recognised by Gandhi, Nehru and Patel. Those Hindu communalists who abuse Gandhi and Nehru most vehemently do not recognise this reality, and this is even more painful.

To understand the true nature of Muslim communalism in India, it is necessary to study the nature of Islam as a religion. It is equally necessary to study the history of Islam. Muslims believe Islam to be the latest and therefore the most perfect religion. They regard Muhammad as the last and the final Prophet. Therefore they believe that there cannot be any new religion after the advent of Islam. They think it is unnecessary to embrace even a chronologically new and more modern faith. They believe that Islam does not need any modification. These Islamic dogmas do not suffer from the restrictions admitted by other religions. When Muslims believe Islam to be perfect and immutable, their faith does not extend to a purely theological domain. Islam has not merely given a theology; it has also given its followers a complete social and political system. Islam has laid down the principles on which the relations between Muslims and infidels are based. An average Muslim who is orthodox in his views fully subscribes to all these dogmas. Some Muslims like Maulana Moududi and Maulana Abul Hassan Nadvi have even discovered an Islamic economic system in addition to these! Today Maulana Moududi and Maulana Nadvi have a very large following among Indian Muslims, and this can hardly be ignored.

Thus the Muslim mind is still under the spell of mediaeval faith. This happens to the followers of any religion for some time. In every religious group, one finds such hardcore orthodoxy which clings to obsolete traditions. But one also finds that in the Hindu as well as the Christian society there emerged a class of reformers who rejected

such dogmas outright. There are reasons for this. Their
religions were subjected to some attacks. Both Christians
and Hindus had to face Islamic aggression. The defeats
they suffered stimulated these societies to reform themselves. Muslim society is unfortunate in this regard. It has
never been subjected to the traumatic experience of an
attack which would later activate it to reform itself.

When I refer to the attacks to which the Christian and
Hindu societies were subjected, I am not referring merely
to political aggression in a limited sense; even Muslims
have been subjected to such attacks. The Muslim community has sometimes been enslaved by aggressors. And
yet its religion has never been threatened. On the other
hand, whenever the Muslims defeated the Christians and
the Hindus they did not stop at enslaving them politically;
they tried to convert them forcibly to Islam. The followers
of other faiths thus realized that if Muslims enslaved
them, their religion was in danger. This is what compelled these societies to think of their own religion in a
radically new manner.

Muslims have often been enslaved by others. In India,
Hindus have often defeated Muslims and ruled over them.
But Hindus did not force Muslims to embrace Hinduism.
Even Shivaji, who could have successfully done so, did
not attempt it. When some Christians defeated
Muslims, they had already given up the idea of forcible
conversion and Christian society was already entering the
modern age. When Christians were not modern, even they
have forcibly converted Muslims to their own faith. Spain
is an example. But this is the only exception to the rule.
When the Turkish Empire started disintegrating, and
when the Western nations started grabbing it piece by
piece, they took over Muslim territory as imperialists and
colonialists. They did not try to spread their religion. It

was not their intention to conquer the Muslims in order to convert them to the Christian faith.

In short, when the Turks captured Constantinopole they renamed it and called it Istanbul. They tore down its Church and built a mosque over it. Christian citizens in the Byzantine Empire were converted to Islam. When the Moguls annexed a new territory in India, the first thing they did was to demolish the temple in each conquered village. This was followed by a forcible conversion of some citizens to Islam. Aurangzeb destroyed the temple of *Vishweshevara* at Banaras, and built a mosque at the birth place of Lord Krishna at Mathura. But the Western con- querers of Mecca and Medina did not inflict any changes of this type on the conquered. The Mosque of Omar in Jerusalem remained intact and Muslim faith remained intact. Muslims were fortunate even when they were ruled by others to have full religious freedom. In India, a king like Shivaji pushed back aggressors and yet he made grants for the preservation of Pirs and Dargahs. But history has taken such absurd twists and turns that it has left the Muslim mind still mediaeval in its make-up. It has never shocked Muslims into an awareness of modernity. Indeed, one is inclined to blame history more than the Muslims themselves for this phenomenon!

However, this fact has had many significant consequen- ces. Muslims have been destroyed and Muslims have been ruled by others, but Muslim society has not been destroyed. When a society survives, it can free it- self from the shackles of alien domination. It can reesta- blish a state of its own. In this context, it must be remem- bered that the Muslim notion of freedom and dependence are not related to, or even consistent with, the modern concept of nationalism. Independence, according to the Muslims, is synonynous with all power being concentrated in the hands of the Muslim community. It is in this sense that they regard Pakistani Muslims as free and Indian Muslims as still in bondage. Indian Muslims believe themselves to be like the Muslims in Mecca and they believe that the Muslims in Pakistan are like the Muslims in Medina. Before the Prophet Muhammad conquered Mecca, Muslims in Mecca had to suffer persecution at the hands of the Quraish tribe. On the other hand, Medina was under Muslim rule. When Muhammad captured Mecca, the Muslims in Mecca were emancipated. I suspect that at least 75 per cent of the rural Muslim population in India believes itself to be in the same position as the Muslims in Mecca before the Prophet's triumphant arrival.

At the time of the last general election, I accompanied a Muslim friend of mine who was contesting the election on his election tour. I met a gentleman there who said, "What do you have this election propaganda for? Why have elections at all? Ayub Khan will soon come over here and put a stop to all this"! I did not lose my temper when I heard this. The gentleman who expressed these views was illiterate. However, I was sad to find a concrete example of the Muslim mind still unfortunately under the spell of obsolete, mediaeval notions. It was poor consolation for me to understand the apparent foolishness of his hopes.

This kind of mediaeval thinking is characteristic of Indian Muslims. In Pakistan, the process of modesnization appears to have made a beginning. However, in India the Muslim community is obsessed with its minority status to such an extent that it tries and succeeds in preventing any process which would modernize themselves. It appears that all so-called secular political parties in India are agreed upon keeping Indian Muslims in their mediaeval state. The Congress party has, in fact, shown that it is opposed to the modernization of Indian Muslims. The reasons for this policy are to be found in the nature of the Muslim leadership within the Congress party. This leadership mostly consists of the orthodox and traditionalist *ulema*. The *ulema* still exert a powerful influence on the senior leadership within the Congress party. It is hardly surprising that our political and administrative leadership, which seeks advice from Muslim leaders who still retain their mediaeval attitude, cannot modernize the Muslim community. Islam in India is Islam in its crudest form: that is why pan-Islamic movements exist in India. This is also the reason why whenever the Prophet is criticized, Muslims in India start movements and agitations unparalleled in the rest of the Muslim world. The Khilafat Committee is still stationed in India. The pan-Islamic-minded Muslims in India exert the greatest possible pressure on the government for adopting a policy favourable to the Arabs. Indian Muslims make strong attempts to justify the Islamic pact between Pakistan, Iran, Turkey and Saudi Arabia. And this in spite of the fact that they know the pact to be against Indian interests. Maulana Asad Madni, Secretary of Jamiat-e-Ulema-i-Hind criticizes as 'traitors' all Indian leaders who are against the policy of supporting the Arabs. Madni and other Muslims like him believe that the love of India is the same as the love of all Muslims anywhere. Thus hundreds of thousands of rupees are raised for the Arabs in India and yet, at the same time, a Muslim hero like Abdul Hamid Hasham who fell in the war with Pakistan and won the *Param Veer Chakra*—the highest award for military heroism—is ignored by all Muslim organizations in India.

Indian Muslim leaders perpetually complain that they are denied religious freedom in India. They claim that the Hindu majority in India treats them with injustice. They fail to realize that their definition of Islam is twisted and strange, for these leaders believe that the greatest injustice to Indian Muslims is the simple fact that there is a majority of Hindus in this country.

5

STRANGE BEDFELLOWS: COMMUNISTS' INTIMACY WITH COMMUNALISTS

Muslim communalists in India and Indian communists have always remained strange, but inseparable, bedfellows. Many people are perplexed by this unusually intimate relationship between those who claim to believe in the Marxist dictum, 'Religion is the opium of the people' and see social change in terms of dialectic processes in history, and Muslim communalists in India.

In fact, this intimacy is not at all surprising. There are significant resemblances between the communist movement and the Muslim communalist movement. First, both movements are international in scope and character. Both aim at establishing an ideological state and neither cares for the means employed in achieving its end. However, their purpose and the processes by which they achieve their objectives are different. As regards the communists, first there is the emergence of the international communist movement in a country. This movement seeks to establish a state. Once the state is established, the movement is directed towards creating the ideal, that is, the Marxist, society. In the case of Muslims the process is just the reverse. A Muslim society already exists. This society seeks to establish its own state. Pakistan is an example of this. In the absence of a Muslim society, a Muslim state cannot be brought into existence.

The basis of the Islamic movement is not the whole of a society but only the Islamic segment of it. The Islamic movement can establish its own state only by subjugating, if not destroying, the other parts of society. For instance, if Muslims happen to be in a minority they can establish an Islamic state only by reducing the non-Muslims to the status of a Minority—either by proselytization or by force. Where there already is a Muslim majority, an Islamic state is naturally in existence. No modernist or liberal trends in a truly Islamic state can ever revise its social structure. This crucial difference is likely to be ignored, for instance, in the context of the collaborative attempts of China (a Communist state) and Pakistan (an Islamic state) to precipitate chaos in India. Islam is a religion and therefore the elimination of other religious beliefs is a necessary precondition for an Islamic state. And no social change in such a state would ever bring about a restoration of the former composition of society. An Islamic state may change. It may even become a secular state. But even this secular state would be the secular government of and by a Muslim majority, in which non-Muslims would have little or no place.

It would also be worthwhile to note the significant resemblances between the communist and the Islamic movement. The communists believe that Islam was the first religion to bring about social equality. In fact, it is the claim to social equality that links both these doctrines. (Did Islam in fact bring about social equality? What is the nature of social equality in Islam? Such questions arise in this context, but they will have to be dealt with separately.) It is assumed that neither movement is nationalistic in character. When communists are not in power, they are internationalists; when Muslims are a minority in any country they lack a nationalistic spirit and have an internationalistic, that is, pan-Islamic, attitude. When either the communists or the Islamists are faced with a choice between modern, territorial nationalism and allegiance to the state on the one hand, and their own international ideology on the other, most of them invariably choose the latter. In short, a communist, when not in power, is primarily an internationalist and only secondarily, if at all, a nationalist. A Muslim in minority is primarily a Muslim and only secondarily, if at all, a nationalist. Both Muslims and communists regard their own concept of social structure as perfect. Both reject freedom of thought. What is even more significant is the fact that both employ strikingly similar methods of propaganda against their opponents. The communists usually dismiss their opponents merely by calling them "stooges of the imperialists" (the current vogue is to brand them all as "agents of the C.I.A."). Indian Muslims, when they criticize another Indian Muslim, call him an "agent" or "stooge" of the Hindus! * Currently, Chairman Mao brands Russian communists as "revisionists". In the Koran when Muhammad discusses the messages of earlier Messiahs such as Moses and Jesus, he criticizes them as 'impure' due to 'revisions'.

The resemblances between these two movements do not end at this point. As soon as they come to power, communists suddenly change from internationalism to extreme nationalism. Instead of decentralizing power, they pursue a policy of strengthening and further centralizing power. The same happens within the course of the Islamic move-

---

* For instance, Maulana Azad. I too have been dubbed a 'Sanghist Muslim' in an editorial by *Radiance*, the weekly organ of the Jamaat-e-Islami.

ment. Most nations with a Muslim majority are extremely
nationalistic in their social and political outlook. In pre-
partition India, the Muslim League used to demand greater
provincial autonomy. But as soon as Pakistan was created,
all remnants of autonomy were totally eliminated. Although
all Arab nations have a common history, tradition and language, they fail to unite. Communists purge their opponents no sooner than they come to power. Muslim nationalistic movements, wherever there is a Muslim majority, do
not allow non-Muslims to exist freely and equally. A clear
example of this is provided by the forced exodus of non-
Muslims from Pakistan. But this phenomenon is not limited
to Pakistan. Every Muslim nation state, with the exception
of Turkey and Indonesia, treats minorities as unequals.
Even Arab nationalism is no exception to this. In fact, Arab
nationalism is not even Islamic nationalism. It is racist.
Arabs believe that being Arab is being the most perfect
Muslim and to them "Islamic" means "Arabic". In the
Arab world, the political connotations of the terms 'Arab'
and 'Muslim' are identical.

Let us turn now to India. Events in India after 1945
help to explain the communist strategy behind their justification of the demand for Pakistan. Since 1942 the communists had lost the possibility of getting a popular backing due to their dissociation from the struggle for independence. There was hardly any backing to be lost by
them even if they supported the demand for Pakistan. India
was on the verge of becoming independent. The nature of
this independence was, for Indian communists, a matter
of anxious speculation.

Peace had broken out and the cold war had begun. The
Soviet Union and its Western Allies against the Nazi me-
nace had developed a relationship of increasing tension
among themselves. In such a situation, the Indian com-

munists had to speculate whether the ruling party in India
would support the Soviet Union or the West in the cold
war. They decided to back Muslim communalists in order
to precipitate nation-wide disintegration, gain a popular
backing from the Indian Muslims, induce the ruling group
in Pakistan to support Soviet policies, and to benefit from
the general chaos and factional fights in the entire subcontinent. This strategy has proved to be a spectacular failure,
because the assumption on which it was based was wide
off the mark. Pakistan dealt with communists very sternly.
Dr Ashraf and Mr Sajjad Zahir who went to Pakistan from
India to give a momentum to the communist movement
there landed up directly in jail. It took them ten years to
get out of jail and they chose to return to India. Although
Ayub and Kosygin display a most cordial friendship, there
are many communist workers rotting for the last twenty
years in the jails of East Pakistan.

However, during the intervening years Muslim communalists and Indian communists seemed to act almost in
collusion. It was not a mere coincidence that the Razakar
movement in Hyderabad and the subversive uprising in
nearby Telangana occurred at about the same time.

When the CPI accepted the Ranadive policy of nation-
wide subversion and uprising, many eminent Muslim League leaders throughout India suddenly became 'communists'! The well-known Assamese writer Abdul Malik, the
editor of the Urdu weekly (and a fellow-traveller) *Siyasat*
published from Hyderabad—Abid Ali—Maulana Ishaq
Shambli of U.P., Mohammed Iliyas of West Bengal, and
Dr Ghani are some of the more glaring examples of this
phenomenon.

The year 1947 saw the dissolution of the Muslim League
in India. Most of its leaders went to Pakistan. Communal
riots shook India and the Hindus developed a feeling of

strong abhorrence towards Muslim communalism. Muslim communalists chose to change their strategy under these circumstances. Some pretended that they had given up their communalism and joined the Congress. The idea was to protect Muslim interests from within the ruling party. Mr A. K. Hafizka of Bombay, for example, is such a recruit. Those who did not relish compromises of this type decided to continue with their subversive tactics under a more acceptable label, knowing that Hindus would react adversely to open expressions of Muslim communalism. They were attracted towards communism not because they embraced the Marxist ideology but because the communist strategy of permanent subversion was congenial and appeared useful to them.

Indian communists, however, have continued to practice double-dealing in relation to Indian Muslims. Their acrobatics make an interesting study in itself. It offers the student of this strange bed-fellowship rich and detailed material. In fact, this love affair is still thriving in spite of the basic incompatability between the objectives of communism and of Muslim communalism. All is fair, perhaps, in love, war, communism, and communalism!

6

MUSLIM OPPOSITION TO
SECULAR INTEGRATION
NATURE, CAUSES AND REMEDIES

Secularism implies a dissociation of religious considerations from political and social life. The modern view of man and society includes a secular attitude to all political and social activities. It does not insist on abolishing religion altogether but regards religion as a matter of personal faith. The ethical values on which modern secular society is based are secular ethical values which are rationally derived. Religions may or may not contain a notion of fundamental human rights as we understand them today. As modern men, we do not rely on religion for deriving our concept of social conscience. Our social conscience is inherent in the democratic system of government we have accepted. The democratic ethic is liberal and is therefore heterodox. It is thus necessary for a democracy to be secular, that is, totally dissociated from religion, to be a democracy at all. All communities and individuals in a democratic society have to conform to the basic liberal democratic ethic.

In many instances, we witness an inevitable conflict between human rights and religion-based social attitudes. In such a situation, the only choice we have as modern democrats is to eliminate the obstacles to democracy created by certain religious attitudes. The very fact that in India we call Muslims a minority and Hindus the majority implies a non-secular attitude. Yet all political parties seem to regard this as a proper division. A secular distinction between people would be in the nature of a class distinction. For instance, a leader of the working class is a secular leader; a leader of Hindus or Muslims is not.

Secularism in India, although embodied in the Constitution, is as yet only an aspiration. It has not yet permeated our social life. It is even in danger today. Within the Hindu majority, there is a strong obscurantist revivalist movement against which we find a very small class of liberals engaged in fight. Among Indian Muslims there is no such liberal minority leading the movement towards democratic liberalism. Unless Indian liberals, however small they are as a minority, are drawn from all communities and join forces on a secular basis, even the Hindu liberal minority will eventually lose its battle with communalist and revivalist Hindus. If Muslims are to be integrated in the fabric of a secular and integrated Indian society, a necessary precondition is to have a class of Muslim liberals who would continuously assail communalist dogmas and tendencies. Such Muslim liberals, along with Hindu liberals and others, would comprise a class of modern Indian liberals.

Liberal intellectuals emerge in any society only through a long and complex social, cultural, political, and historical process. Today Hindus have an influential liberal élite only because Hinduism is historically heterodox and can accommodate dissent. The modern Indian liberal tradition starts from Raja Rammohan Roy, who was a product of Hindu society. It leads through such secular (as against

Hindu) liberals as Nehru to the present time.

The target of Hindu liberals has been Hindu orthodoxy. And due to their continuous critical evaluation and leadership in social reform, Hindu society as a whole has been benefited to a certain extent. I do not wish to suggest here that Hindu society has accepted the liberal democratic ethic and has modernized itself to any satisfactory extent; it has not. But this continuing liberal tradition places the Hindu community in a culturally better position than that of Muslims in India.

Why do Muslims in India lack a liberal elite? The answer has many facets. But one thing is certain. The explanation of Muslim backwardness is to be found in the very make-up of the Muslim mind.

Indian Muslims believe that they are a perfect society and are superior to all other communities in India. One of the grounds for this belief is the assumption that the Islamic faith embodies the vision of a perfect society and, therefore, being a perfect Muslim implies not having to make any further progress. This is an unacceptable claim by modern criteria.

Islamic personal law runs contrary to the modern notions of human rights. Its anomalies are obvious to anyone except Muslim males and need not be detailed here.

The second reason for this belief is the fact that Indian Muslims resent being a minority and still dream of spreading their faith throughout India or at least of ruling India. They suffer from delusions of grandeur and also from a persecution mania. I can cite a number of examples of this from the Muslim press in India and the statements of Leaders of the Jamaat-e-Islami and the Majlis-e-Mushawarat. Another reason for this belief is found in the prepartion history of Muslim politics in India. Muslims have always believed that they are a state within a state and a society within a society. Their ideas of representation are based on this claim and therefore they run contrary to the concept of a democratic society itself. Today they believe in a parallel co-existence with the majority with complete autonomy as a community. This explains their resistance to a change in their personal law. But, going even further, Indian Muslims oppose family planning because they are obsessed with the idea of increasing their numbers to be effective in power politics. This is the same old dangerous attitude as led to the demand for, and creation of, Pakistan. Their sense of loyalty to Pakistan, that is, their view of the Kashmir problem and their defence of infiltrators in States like Assam, is another aspect of this anti-secular view. Their failure to identify themselves as Indians becomes obvious in these and many other ways.

The only leadership Indian Muslims have is basically communalist. An exceptional Muslim liberal like M. C. Chagla has no place in Indian Muslim society. Nor will individual modern liberals suffice. Indian Muslims today need an *avant garde* liberal élite to lead them. This élite must identify itself with other modern liberals in India and must collaborate with it against Muslim as well as Hindu communalism. Unless a Muslim liberal intellectual class emerges, Indian Muslims will continue to cling to obscurantist medievalism, communalism, and will eventually perish both socially and culturally. A worse possibility is that of Hindu revivalism destroying even Hindu liberalism, for the latter can succeed only with the support of Muslim liberals who would modernize Muslims and try to impress upon them secular democratic ideals.

I believe that the only remedy to Muslim communalism is an enlightened liberal intellectual leadership. This leadership, to have credibility and persuasive power, must emerge from amongst the Indian Muslims themselves. The

first task of such a liberal leadership would be to destroy
the hold of communalist leadership over Indian Muslim
masses. The influence of organizations such as the Jamaat-
e-Islami, the Majlis-e-Mushawarat and Tamir-e-Millat has
to be eliminated. So-called 'nationalist' Muslims, who are
basically communalist, must be exposed. Also, Muslims
who are today leaders of political parties such as the Right
Communist but who like Mr Mohammed Iliyas of West
Bengal are proven communalists, must be exposed. The
ulema must be prevented from propagating anti-national
ideas in the name of religion. The communalist Muslim
press must be rendered ineffective. In short, the pervasive
influence of all kinds of communalists has to be rendered
ineffective.

There are some Muslims who are members of the Indian
élite but who are afraid of their own community's reaction
to modern attitudes. These uncommitted and hypocritical
liberals are not only of no use, but are also a hindrance
to the progress of Indian Muslims. They are either moral
cowards or are apathetic to a great social problem which
is also a problem of democracy in India. They must make
a choice now. If they do not provide liberal intellectual
leadership to Indian Muslims, the younger generation has
to commit itself and carry out this task.

It is often argued that Muslim communalism is only a
reaction to Hindu communalism. This is not true. The real
conflict in India today is between all types of obscurantism, dogmatism, revivalism, and traditionalism on one side
and modern liberalism on the other. Indian politicians being short-sighted and opportunistic, communalism and orthodoxy is always appeased and seldom, if ever, opposed.
This is why we need an agreement among all liberal intellectuals to create a non-political movement against all
forms of communalism. If this is not done, democracy and

liberalism will inevitably collapse in India. The stakes are high. It is a pity that few people realize the gravity of the situation. It is even more unfortunate that they are hardly informed about the true nature of the problem.

7

HUMANISTIC MODERNISM
THE ONLY SOLUTION

In the preceding chapters I have discussed the nature of the Indian Muslim problem. In this context, one ought to consider Hindu communalism. However, I believe that Hindu communalism in India has sprung up primarily as a reaction to Muslim communalism. If Muslim communalism is effectively eliminated, the root cause of Hindu communalism will be destroyed.

This is not the only reason why I consider these two forms of communalism on different levels. As I have stated earlier, the Hindu community already has within it an influential liberal élite which is conscious of fundamental human values and is committed to them. This small but influential class of liberals continuously fights Hindu communalism. Such a liberal élite does not exist among the Indian Muslims. This is the chief reason why I do not regard the two communalist forces as being on the same level. Basically, Muslim communalism is aggressive and expansionist; Hindu communalism is a defensive reaction. However hard Hindu communalist leaders may try, they cannot make Hindu communalism aggressive beyond certain limits. By its very nature, Hindu society is not well-knit. Liberal Hindus are well organised and they are con-

tinuously trying to check aggressive communalism. Even
during the post-partition days when communal feelings
ran high, Hindu communalists could not subjugate the
forces of secular nationalism among the Hindus.

However, the Hindu assumes various forms. It will be
useful to study the Hindu mind in contrast with the Muslim mind. Hindu society allows free expression. This opens
out a certain inlet for new and different ideas. A Hindu
can take up extremely wrong positions at times and even
try to propagate highly non-conformist views. Such a
wrong-headed Hindu can even muster up some support.
As a result, we simultaneously find among the Hindus
people who are extremely tolerant and humanistic and
also others who are extremely cruel and narrow-minded.
The Hindu wears many masks. In a sense, Hindu society
is a multi-headed organism. Sometimes this creates great
complications. It also explains the indecision and the
ambivalence of the Hindu mind. It postpones decisions
and avoids frankness. At the same time, it tries to obtain
full credit for its independence of mind.

Of course, there is another side to this. This other side
is equally important in the context of Muslim politics and
the Hindu-Muslim problem. As I have observed earlier,
Gandhi and Nehru had recognised the fact that Hindu
society had refused to accept the Muslim challenge. But
Hindu communalists failed to recognise this. I must
observe here that Hindu society lacks the dynamism without which no national challenge can be faced. For centuries it has been in the doldrums. It is yet to find a direction. I am not referring to the controversies raging in this
country today. The real question is whether we have
enough dynamism and sense of direction to overcome
these controversies. American society has such dynamism
and so too the Russian. In comparison to the Russians and

Americans, the Europeans are losing their dynamism. And therefore, they are being left behind. It must be remembered that dynamic nations go on extending the spheres of their influence. Sometimes they may expand geographically; sometimes, their expansion is cultural; and sometimes their influence spreads in the form of economic and political influence. Today, India is a shrinking nation in this sense and this points to the lack of dynamism in a majority of Indians. It is not the leadership alone which is responsible for this waning of influence. English society overthrew Chamberlain to prove how a dynamic society can reject weak leadership. However, even in periods of difficulty we have been unable to overthrow our weak leadership. Our leadership is merely a symbol of the weakness of Indian society as a whole.

Does Muslim society then have such dynamism? The answer is, 'No.' We have recently witnessed how Arab power shrank up within only twenty-four hours. Nowhere in the world today do we find a dynamic influence of Islamic culture. These are the symptoms of a debilitated society. Islamic dynamism is preoccupied only with spreading religion. Muslims call this dynamism; in fact, it is only a hang-over of barbaric mediaevalism and it contains the seeds of its own destruction.

How then are we going to explain the spectacle of the Hindus' helplessness in the face of Indian Muslims? The creation of Pakistan cannot be attributed to Muslim dynamism. Pakistan was created by the Muslims in collusion with a third party. It is a sealed chapter now. However, the conflict continues. It is a conflict of two attitudes. The Muslim mind is basically expansionist because it dreams of religious expansion. The Hindu is conservative. He would not transcend self-imposed limitations. This habit of the Hindu is sometimes expressed in an absurd form.

He decides not to enter Kashmir which is a part of his own nation. He refuses to allow everyone, including himself, to enter Naga territory. These are symptoms of decadence.

When I talk of expansionism, I should not be misunderstood as its advocate. I am not suggesting that a society ought to be expansionist. After all, the modern conscience provides a yard-stick to determine what kind of expansion is ethically justifiable. I expect a dynamic Hindu society of the future to develop a modern conscience. I believe that if the Hindus were sufficiently dynamic, the Hindu-Muslim problem would be solved. For if the Hindus were dynamic, they would subject the Indian Muslims to several shocks which history has spared them. Muslims would be left with the one stark alternative to perish if they did not wish to change. And any society prefers change to extinction. Hindus can accept the challenge of Muslim politics in India only by developing dynamism and a balance of mind. But to develop such dynamism Hindu orthodoxy itself has to be liquidated. The caste system has to be eliminated. The Hindus must embrace modernism. They must create a society based on fundamental human values and the concept of true social equality. Unfortunately, the Hindu mind lacks balance. Even those Hindus who have accepted modernity, justice and brotherhood as their guiding principles sometimes support Muslim communalism. Some avoid speaking against it and some even indirectly encourage it. Those Hindus who ought to be combating communalism today seem, instead, to be trying to put the clock back. They are supporting obscurantism, revivalism, the caste system and the cult of the cow. This is a process which would drain Hindu society of whatever little dynamism it may still have. There have to be enough Hindus trying to modernize the Hindu society and, at the same time, op-

posing the irrational politics of Muslim communalism. I
hope this would happen. For that would precisely be the
process by which the Hindu-Muslim problem can be eliminated. Muslim communalism today makes the most of
the rift between liberal Hindus and communalist Hindus.
It is ironical that Muslim communalists gain the support
of Hindus, both liberal and communalist. The Muslim
communalist demand for making Urdu a second official
language in Uttar Pradesh and Bihar has been supported
by the so-called modernist Hindu under the impressive
label of secularism. The 'secularism' of such Hindus encourages the anti-secularism of the Muslims. These so-
called secularist Hindus are opposed to the creation of a
common personal law because it might displease the Muslims. They support Sheikh Abdulla and suggest measures
which are bound to result in giving Kashmir over to Pakistan to settle our disputes with that country. When members of the Jamaat-e-Islami are arrested for demonstrating
against President Nasser in New Delhi, these 'secularist'
Hindus promptly protest. They back the Muslim agitation against the Bharatiya Vidya Bhavan, publishers of the
controversial book on the Prophet. When Hamid Dalwai's
novel *Indhan* ('Fuel') raises a storm of protest from Muslim fanatics, these so-called Hindu secularists would support the fanatics and oppose Hamid Dalwai. When Mr
Chagla attempts to straighten up the communalist twist
given to the Aligarh University issue, under the pretence
of being anti-Congress the secularist Hindus would just
sit on the fence. Such, in short, are the ways of the so-
called secular Hindu.

Consider, next, the orthodox Hindu. He stages an agitation against the proposed removal of the word 'Hindu'
from Banares University, and secures the support of the
Muslim League. He would start an agitation for a ban on

cow-slaughter and Muslim communalists would support even that. For when they support him on such issues, both of them can establish a united front against Mr Chagla, and then the Muslim communalist would also be left free to stage nation-wide agitations for a re-display of the Prophet's lost hair. He can bully critics of the Prophet. In short, he will always turn Hindu revivalism to his own benefit. It must be remembered that the obscurantism of one community helps to strengthen the obscurantism of other communities. If Hindu obscurantism is attacked and eliminated, it would also be a strong blow to Muslim obscurantism.

Who then is really fighting Muslim communalism? The answer is, a handful of modern Muslims. Mr Chagla in fact leads the modern liberal Muslims. And all of us know Mr Chagla's situation now. He is opposed by the Muslims and unsupported by the Hindus.

There is no doubt that the picture I have painted of Indian Muslims is terrible. But it is true. One would be deceiving oneself if one tried to believe it was otherwise.

This, however, is what we observe on the surface. On the surface, Muslim society appears to be mediaeval in its make-up. Yet, somewhere deep down, a change is taking place in this society. There is nothing dramatic about this change. It is largely imperceptible and indeed very slow. It is a process which began quite a few years ago. It has still to cover many stages before it reaches its completion. Sir Syed Ahmed Khan represents the first phase in the modernization of Indian Muslims. He wanted to modernize the Muslims although he was still opposed to the Hindus. Jinnah and Iqbal represent the second phase. In the begin-later they began to talk in the name of Islam and this ning, neither Jinnah nor Iqbal was anti-Hindu. However, Islamism ultimately led to anti-Hinduism. This is where

the process of Muslim modernization was arrested. The
Hindus, on the other hand, had progressed much further.
Raja Rammohun Roy represents the first phase of Hindu
modernism. Many of his views were similar to those later
held by Sir Syed Ahmed Khan. For instance, the Raja, like
Sir Syed, thought that British rule was a divine gift to
India. Savarkar represents the second phase; he wanted
to modernize Hindu society, although he seemed to em-
phasize technological modernity more than scientific outlook out of pragmatic considerations. Nehru represents
the third phase. Nehru was modern in that he was firmly
committed to democracy and the values of an open society.
It is interesting to see that the Hindus had a Savarkar and
a Nehru almost simultaneously. The two phases overlap-
ped. Muslims in India have yet to produce their Nehru or
even Savarkar.

However, a new generation of Muslims is emerging in
India today. One can see the first glimmers of a genuine
modern humanism in them. In the vast mass of a mediaeval
Muslim society one witnesses a few young Muslims who
have a modern, humanistic and rational attitude. They are
still scattered and isolated like islands in a vast ocean.
Their modernity is reflected in what they speak and write.
It is seen in their actions.

It may be useful to cite a few examples. Some educated
Indian Muslims show the signs of a newly emerging attitude of unbiased detachment. For instance, Professor
Mohammad Yasin's book, *Social History of Islamic India*,
Professor Athar Rizvi's work analysing Muslim revivalism
in the 16th and 17th centuries, and Professor M. Mujeeb's book *Indian Muslims*, reveal a new attitude of critical detachment. This kind of modern attitude is also
shared by Professor Mohammad Habib and the Head of
the Department of Political Science at Osmania University,

Dr Rashiduddin Khan. During my recent visit to Aligarh
I had a chance to meet and talk to some men and women
students as well as some of the teaching staff. Even among
them I found the hopeful signs of a critically introspective attitude. In many cities in Northern India not only
is the *purdah* fast disappearing but there is also a rapid
spread of education among Muslim women. Many of these
have married men of other faiths. It is significant to note
that these men of other religions who married Muslim
women were not urged to become Muslims. All these
trends indicate the emergence of modernity among Indian
Muslims.

Are we going to welcome these new trends? Are we
going to encourage them and let them flourish? This is
what we have to decide now. We have to check Pakistani
expansionism and protect our borders. We have to adopt
a clear and decisive long-range policy towards Pakistan.
We have to support Muslim modernism in India. We have
to insist on a common personal law for all citizens of
India. All marriages in India must be registered under a
common Civil Code. Religious conversion should not be
allowed, except when the intending convert is adult and
the conversion takes place before a magistrate. Children
born of inter-religious marriages should be free to practise any religion but only after they reach legal adulthood.
If either a dargah or a temple obstructs the passage of
traffic on a thoroughfare, it ought to be removed. Government should have control over the income of all religious
property. This income should be spent on education and
public welfare alone. It should not be obligatory to mention one's religion and caste (even today, the admission
form used in schools compels students to state their religion). The Banaras and Aligarh Universities should be
declared national institutions of higher learning and their

constitutions should be modified for the purpose. The
special status given to Kashmir should be scrapped. All
Indian citizens should be free to visit Nagaland. There
should be opportunities for the development of Urdu; even
schools which use Urdu as medium of instruction should
have full protection. However, the demand for giving Urdu
the status of the second official language of a State should
be firmly resisted. The status of all Indian women should
be governed by a single, common Civil Code. The *purdah*
should be legally banned. The question of a ban on cow-
slaughter should be settled strictly with reference to the
agricultural and economic development of the country.
Family planning should be made compulsory for all, for
example, by compulsory sterilization of one of the part-
ners after the birth of the third child. Those Muslims who
oppose these reforms should not be entitled to full citizenship rights. For instance, they should have no right of
vote. They should not be eligible for receiving the bene-
fits of any social welfare scheme. Those Muslims who oppose reform on the ground of religion should be governed
strictly according to the *Shariat* law in its entirety. For
example, if they are caught stealing, their hands should
be cut off in public. If they speak a falsehood, they should
be publicly whipped. A Muslim woman who is found
guilty of adultery should be stoned to death in public. I
hope those who insist on following the *Shariat* law will
not indeed find this separate code of crime and punishment
for orthodox Muslims outdated. If so, they should not
seek to apply the *Shariat* only partially.

The only answer to the communal problem in India is
secular integration of all the peoples of India. If the question is viewed in this light, liberal Muslim modernism
would be strengthened. Today we have a suitable climate
for the emergence of a strong modernist movement among

the Muslims. Muslims no more enjoy power. Muslim orthodoxy without power is like a serpent without its poison fangs; only its tail would wriggle. In future we need not discuss the Hindu-Muslim problem. We should discuss a common Civil Code and launch a movement for it.

For all this to happen, the present division among the Hindus should cease to exist. Those Hindus who want to counter Muslim communalism unfortunately try to strengthen Hindu revivalism. And those Hindus who want to lead the Hindus and ultimately the whole of this nation on the way of modernity are unfortunately supporting Muslim communalists. This has to change. I am on the side of all Hindus who oppose Muslim communalism; but when the same Hindus help Hindu revivalism, I am opposed to them. I support all those who want to modernize the Hindus; but when they adopt a policy of not opposing Muslim communalism, I oppose them. If the Hindus develop a proper balance of mind, I believe the present tensions would soon begin to resolve.

THE ANGRY YOUNG SECULARIST

an Interview by

Dilip Chitre

I met Hamid Dalwai twelve years ago in the crowded and musty office of a Marathi literary magazine. At that time he had already made his mark as a short story writer while I, who was younger and practically unknown in literary circles, carried all my unpublished writing on my person. (Since I wrote only poems then, the most portable of literary genres, this was not difficult.) He had already published a brilliant short story called *Kafanchor* (meaning : 'The Shroud-stealer').

He has not, in appearance, changed much since. But if my vague memory is right, he sported a full beard then. I too had a full beard. But his beard was treated with a different sort of significance. Although he spoke Marathi with an authentic Chiplun accent, he was a Muslim. Some of his readers, reading his fluent Marathi, even thought that the name 'Hamid Dalwai' was a pseudonym. This, too, is quite significant. If I remember correctly, when I met him first what drew my attention to him was the fact that another Marathi writer greeted him with the mock-excla-

101

mation "Ya Yavan!" The word 'Yavan' was formerly used
for Greeks, but after the Hindu revival it has been speci-
fically reserved for Muslims, at least in Marathi. A *Yavan*
is a 'bloody foreigner'—an outsider with doubtful creden-
tials. The greeting was jocular, but not insignificant.

During the last twelve years, things have changed for
both of us. I have been generally preoccupied with creative and critical writing. Hamid Dalwai on the other hand
is totally involved in a much more unsafe and urgent social and cultural task. He is working with stupendous in-
tensity on an almost one-man programme to create a modern, secular, and democratic consciousness among Indian
Muslims. So now, in addition to being a *Yavan* to Hindus,
he has achieved the distinction of becoming a *kafir* to orthodox Muslims. He has not entirely given up creative
writing. But today he spends most of his time lecturing to
Hindu and Muslim audiences throughout India. He meets
younger Muslims and talks to them. He engages in all
kinds of debates and polemics. It was he who led the first
morcha ever of Muslim women in Bombay to the Chief
Minister, demanding a modernization of Muslim personal
law. A similar *morcha* in Poona was even greater in size
and impact. Incidentally, the Chief Minister of Maharashtra met the deputationists, but the Prime Minister of India
—a woman herself—refused even to see for a few minutes
the woman leader of the *morcha* in Poona!

Now in his middle thirties, Hamid looks younger than he
is. He is, on principle, clean-shaven now. At one of his
public meetings at Sholapur, he said that if he were in
power he would compel all Muslims to shave off their
beards. Beards have become a community emblem for
some Muslims. It is like those Hindus who still display
their caste-marks in this so-called secular society. However, the next day, at another rally, a shrewd old orthodox

Muslim, referring to Hamid's proposal for a compulsory removal of beards, observed: "We had been told that our friend Mr Hamid Dalwai was a learned man from Bombay. But yesterday, during his discourse, we were taken aback when we discovered that he was only a self-championing barber...!" Hamid himself told me this story, roaring with laughter.

Hamid Dalwai is a self-made man. He does not have a university degree. He comes from an extremely poor family living in a village on the Konkan coast. And yet today he is one of those few young Indians who are action-oriented in a selfless way. He has risked his life and the security of his family.

His last novel, *Indhan* ('Fuel') sparked off a series of explosions in his native village. In the novel, a Maharashtrian young woman—a high-caste Brahmin—attempts to seduce the bachelor protagonist-narrator after having had a long affair with his married elder brother. The protagonist is a Muslim. This really proved to be 'Fuel': the orthodox Muslims in Hamid's village instigated the orthodox Hindus to protest! Together, the entire orthodoxy boycotted and persecuted Hamid's eighty-year old father. Such is the fear of pollution and such are the notions of parallel purity and compartmentalized 'co-existence' in communalist India in the nineteen-sixties. In Bombay, Hamid received anonymous letters threatening the life of his young daughter and his wife, besides his own.

Despite his lack of formal education, he can write and argue very well. He is not an intellectual. But his sincerity distinguishes him anywhere. His human warmth and sense of humour make him an admirable conversationist. He has been a journalist, an active political worker (SSP), and a creative writer. But of late, these things have slid into the background: his central concern is with making the

people around him sane, sober, modern, secular and democratic citizens. And he works. This sets him apart from
intellectual sitters-on-the-fence as well as from political
opportunists of all shades of colour.

I decided to interview him because it is a unique thing,
at least in present-day India, for a promising creative writer to forgo his literary ambition and get involved in social
and cultural action.

When I interviewed Hamid Dalwai recently, he was not
exactly prepared for it. Nor was I. We met at my office—
for, not having a study of his own, Hamid is continuously
in circulation—by previous appointment. It was four o'clock
in the afternoon. The weather was stuffy and uninspiring
as it is just before the monsoon sets in. Hamid walked in
and settled down in front of me and continued to read a
weekly which he had already unfolded. Unsure of how to
begin, I said, "So, I am going to interview you, am I?" He
dropped the paper on the table and winked with his green-
grey eyes.

It is difficult to 'interview' Hamid in the conventional
sense of the term. When he speaks it is a mixture of con-
versation, monologue, and public speaking. His voice has
a terrific volume. And his speaking has a kind of absent-
minded velocity too. So, when he is quite involved, he is
unstoppable. He drowns one's interruptions into the sheer
volume of his own voice. But fortunately, he has the un-
canny knack of anticipating one's next question.

"When did you first start taking Muslim communalism
seriously?", I asked. "I was born in 1932", he began, "in
a Maharashtrian Muslim family. It was in 1946, I think,
when I joined the Rashtra Seva Dal that I was first confronted by the problem. When I joined the Rashtra Seva

Dal, I was the first and only Muslim boy in my village to
do so."

"What was the reaction of your parents and other Muslims?", I asked him.

"Hostile", He said as if I should have known the answer.
"Why?"

"They thought it wasn't the right thing to do. One should
not leave one's own fold. Muslims should stay among Muslims: it is simple!"

"And then? Did you continue?"

"Of course, I did. I couldn't understand why I shouldn't
have done it." Then he paused for a while and said, "Look!
I have got to say some more important things. Let me
finish these autobiographical preliminaries quickly. Are
they necessary at all? Anyway! When I was studying for
my S.S.C. examination, I wrote some articles on Urdu and
the Marathi-speaking Muslims. They were published by a
leading Marathi daily in Bombay. They even provoked
editorial comments." He chuckled and paused again.

"You took to politics quite early, didn't you?", I asked,
taking advantage of the unexpected pause.

"Yes", he said telegraphically, "Congress Socialist Party—
Socialist Party—Praja-Socialist Party—Socialist Party (the
Lohia one)—Samyukta Socialist; that was how it went."

"Are you still with the SSP?" I asked.

"Yes and no!", he said, "I totally disapprove of their line
on communalism."

"In fact, it's a wide rift. The point is, the SSP has failed to
take up a clear, hard line on Muslim communalism."

"Do you see any other party which has?"

"No!" He said, "They are all equally reluctant to undertake the task of real social transformation—which is the
crux of the problem."

"What do you think this task involves?"

"First and foremost, people must be made conscious that there is such a thing as fundamental human values and these must be separated from religious values. This is something which Muslims would never concede because it is claimed that the Koran itself defines fundamental human values perfectly." Here he paused, winked again for effect, and added, "They are as orthodox and anti-modern as the Communists in this respect. Theirs is a closed system."

"Isn't there any liberal tradition among Indian Muslims?" He laughed, "Indian Muslims are, as a rule, liberal only when liberal Hindus blame communalist Hindus." Then he continued in a more serious tone, "Sir Syed Ahmed Khan was a liberal. Today, I can count them on my fingers. Professor Mohammad Habib, the opposition candidate for Vice-Presidency in the last elections, is a liberal. M. C. Chagla is a liberal. Dr Rashiduddin Khan of Osmania University is another liberal I know." His look became a little abstracted, "You know, among Hindus there is a modern, liberal tradition starting from Raja Rammohun Roy. Nehru, in my estimate, was a modern, secular Indian liberal. But he had a tradition behind him. There is no parallel to this among Indian Muslims."

"Why?" I asked.

"Well! It is all there in their history. Muslims were rulers in India for 800 years. And yet they have remained a permanent minority. They strongly resent this. You will find that wherever they are in a minority Muslims always resist secular integration. In India, it is worse. The *ulema* still dream of a *Dar-ul-Islam* in this sub-continent. That was why they opposed partition, not because they were interested in secular Indian nationalism. Those who implicitly accepted the fact that Muslims would remain a permanent minority in the sub-continent demanded Pakistan and got it. But those who still remain here dream of a 'deliverer'—which is an illusion, almost a sickness. Now while the *ulema* sided with the Congress in opposing partition, after partition they still continue to champion a separate Muslim identity: a parallel society within the Indian society that will have the least possible to do with non-Muslims. Mentally, they still live in a mediaeval world. And they do not realize that this makes them misfits in the modern world."

"How do Indian Muslims react to 'Muslims' like you?"

"Well! To most of them I am a sort of a *kafir*, an infidel!"

"How then do you expect to have an impact on them?"

"I have hopes. For instance, Muslim girls and women in India do show an awareness of the inequities of Muslim personal law. But this is a difficult task, I mean the task of secular integration. No political party in India is forthright enough to take steps towards eradicating communalism. They appease the Muslims. My own party—the SSP —is no exception. There has to be a non-party organization to tackle the problem. We have made a small beginning in this direction in the form of Indian Secular Forum."

"What is the response?"

"Not very encouraging, except that a few dedicated people have joined us. Some have come up with financial help. But financially, we are very badly off."

"How do you work?"

"Ah!", he said, "I move about, talk to people, try to make them think and argue. I write articles too."

"What about your creative writing?"

"It will look after itself, I suppose, when the need arises!" He said, "Right now, this is all that is bothering me: political parties have failed to solve the problem. The National Integration Convention was just a joke. People come up with mere platitudes. Nobody tries to go to the root of the problem."

"What about the Hindu liberals you spoke of?"

"Even they will be eventually swallowed up by Hindu revivalism and Muslim revivalism which seem to be acting, ironically, in collusion. If secular democratic ideals are to survive, all liberal forces in this country have to rally and work together on a non-party, non-political basis!" He paused and added, finally, "One can't helplessly watch the game. The rules have to change."

INDEX